Refugees in Our Own Land

Refugees in Our Own Land

Chronicles from a Palestinian Refugee Camp in Bethlehem

Muna Hamzeh

Pluto Press

LONDON • STERLING, VIRGINIA

First published 2001 by Pluto Press
345 Archway Road, London N6 5AA
and 22883 Quicksilver Drive,
Sterling, VA 20166–2012, USA

www.plutobooks.com

British Library Cataloguing in Publication Data
A catalogue record for this book is available from the British Library

ISBN 0 7453 1652 2 hardback

Library of Congress Cataloging in Publication Data
Hamzeh, Muna, 1959-
   Refugees in our own land : chronicles from a Palestinian refugee
camp in Bethlehem / Muna Hamzeh.
      p. cm.
   ISBN 0–7453–1652–2 (hard : alk. paper)
   1. Al-Aqsa Intifada, 2000—Personal narratives. 2. Hamzeh, Muna,
1959– .—Diaries. 3. Palestinian American journalists—Diaries. 4.
Refugees, Palestinian Arab—West Bank—Duhayshah (Refugee camp)—
Social conditions.   I. Title.
   DS119.765 .H36 2001
   956.95'3—dc21

                                                     2001002266

Designed and produced for Pluto Press by
Chase Publishing Services, Fortescue, Sidmouth EX10 9QG
Typeset from disk by Stanford DTP Services, Northampton
Printed in the European Union by TJ International, Padstow, England

Contents

Dedication

Between 1990 and 2000, the years I lived in Dheisheh, three people never ceased to urge me and encourage me to write a book. They are my dear friends Marianne Weiss in Paris, Sami Kamal in Jerusalem and Mira Hamermesh in London. I thank them for believing in me.

When I kept an email diary during the first two months of al-Aqsa Intifada (September–November 2000), hundreds of readers sent me touching electronic messages from Japan, Jordan, Sweden, Pakistan, Canada, Syria, the United Kingdom, Lebanon, France, Egypt, Italy, Iran, the United States, to name some. There was even an email from Princess Haya bint al-Hussein (daughter of the late King Hussein of Jordan). Without these messages of support, I couldn't have kept on writing the diary. To each and every one of these wonderful people, I say thank you for supporting and encouraging me.

Of course, *Refugees in Our Own Land* would never have been written had it not been for the refugees of Dheisheh, female and male, young and old. They embraced me as one of their own and made me feel at home, from the moment I married and lived in the camp in the summer of 1990. My friends, in-laws, neighbors, and acquaintances opened up my eyes to the real life story of Palestinians in the camps. They taught me, by their sheer existence, that not only are the refugees in the camps the least understood segment of Palestinian society, but also that they are the ones who will one day lead our people to full independence and liberation.

But the biggest thank you goes to my former husband, Ahmed Muhaisen. Had it not been for Ahmed, I would not have lived in Dheisheh for one day, let alone for ten years. And had it not been for Ahmed's love and support, I would never have come to regard Dheisheh as my only true home; the one place where I'll always feel I have family.

Muna Hamzeh
Austin, Texas
May 2001

Preface

"We hold these truths to be self-evident, that all men are created equal, that they are endowed by their Creator with certain unalienable Rights, that among these are Life, Liberty and the pursuit of Happiness."

From the U.S. Declaration of Independence – July 4, 1776

Right from the start I must confess that this book was not easy to complete. I suppose that if I were still residing in Dheisheh, the Palestinian refugee camp that is the subject of this work, then the task at hand would have been easier, both emotionally and psychologically. But sitting here in Austin, Texas, tens of thousands of miles away from Dheisheh, I must admit that the pain of writing about the refugee camp that I have grown to love so much has taken its toll on me. At times, I know it is my intense longing for Dheisheh that overwhelms me. Other times, I know it is the indifference of the world to the continuing suffering of the Palestinians that pains me. But all the time, I do know that my biggest source of anguish is accepting the fact that Dheisheh is a chapter in my life that has come to a full close. Coming to terms with this fact does not leave me happy. And how can it, when Dheisheh and the nearly 10,000 men, women and children who live there, have unintentionally taken an incredibly big slice of my heart, and kept it. And so I know now for certain that I shall never get over Dheisheh. Ever!

For those who don't know it, Dheisheh Refugee Camp lies less than two miles south of the Church of the Nativity in Bethlehem, where Jesus Christ was born. It is one of 59 Palestinian refugee camps established in the West Bank, the Gaza Strip, Syria, Lebanon and Jordan after the 1948 Arab–Israeli War, which led to the expulsion of nearly 700,000 Palestinians from their homes, and resulted in the longest-running refugee problem in the world. Dheisheh is one of 20 refugee camps in the West Bank, and the largest of three camps in Bethlehem. Most of the 40 villages from which Dheisheh's refugees originally came were located near Hebron and Jerusalem, in areas that are now part of Israel. After 1948, Israel destroyed all these villages and built Israeli colonies in their place. Dheisheh's refugees, who had been farmers accustomed to living on a total of about 125,000 acres of privately owned land, 5,000 of which were planted with olive trees, suddenly found themselves squeezed together in a small, overcrowded camp. Today, Dheisheh's nearly 10,000 refugees live on a tiny 90-acre stretch of land.

To some outsiders, Dheisheh may, of course, be nothing more than a squalid and poverty-stricken Palestinian refugee camp. To others, it is living proof of the immense and ongoing tragedy imposed on the Palestinians since the creation of the State of Israel in 1948. But for me, Dheisheh is the only place I've ever lived in where I felt completely at home. In the past 41 years, I have lived first in the West Bank, then in Jordan, then in the USA, then in the West Bank again, and now in the United Sates again. And yet, I have never felt that I could call a place home like I can call Dheisheh. I say this because Dheisheh's closely-knit community embraced me with open arms and gave me a feeling that I lacked all my life – the feeling that I was part of a family. And this makes leaving the camp all the more difficult.

But the refugee camp did more than just make me feel part of a family. It also opened my eyes to the real plight of the Palestinian refugees in the camps. Poverty, damp and closely clustered houses, meager living conditions, overcrowding in the schools, unpaved roads and poor infrastructure are only part of the hardships that the refugees in the camps have to endure on a daily basis and have had to endure for the past 53 years. Yet in the midst of all this difficulty, families thrive, children are born, weddings and funerals take place, parents work and a mini-society grapples to find itself a warm place under the sun.

Between 1990 and 2000 when I lived in Dheisheh, some Western TV crews would seek my help whenever they came to do one story or another about the refugees. The shots they looked for focused on children with torn and dirty clothes, or impoverished dwellings, or any other image that depicted the refugees as those "poor", "miserable" and "wretched" souls. They never even attempted to scratch the surface and what was lost in all this are the images of the camp as a place that is free of crime, a place where you can step out and leave your front door open. Also lost is the image of the mothers who take good care of their children and are kind to the elderly, and help a friend if she is bed-ridden after surgery. But mostly what is lost is the spirit of a people who have refused to succumb to injustice, and who have refused to give up their right to return to their villages, no matter how many years have gone by.

When the West Bank, and therefore Dheisheh, was ruled by Jordan between 1948 and 1967, Dheisheh's refugees were often placed under curfew following demonstrations calling for the end of Jordanian rule. Anti-Jordanian demonstrations were commonplace as was the Jordanian army's brutality in trying to suppress these demonstrations. In the 1950s and 1960s, several refugees from Dheisheh spent time in Jordanian jails as political prisoners. When Israel occupied the West Bank, East Jerusalem and the Gaza Strip in 1967, matters only became worse. Scores of Dheisheh's refugees were killed by Israeli troops, hundreds were wounded, hundreds more were imprisoned, scores were deported and scores more had their homes either demolished or sealed by the Israeli military. Yet the spirit to resist the occupation never subsided, not even slightly.

This year marks 53 years since the expulsion of the Palestinians from their homes, and 52 years since the inception of Dheisheh as a refugee camp. Yet today, we aren't any closer to a political solution to the refugee problem, nor to the Palestinian–Israeli conflict as a whole. Yet the need for a just and peaceful solution to the biggest quagmire of the twentieth century – which now has spilled over into the twenty-first century, has never been more vital. Since the start of the second Palestinian uprising on September 29, 2000, Israel's military and settlers have killed 484 Palestinians, including 13 Israeli Arabs and two refugees at Lebanon's northern border; and have injured 13,591 Palestinians, including 1,500 with permanent disabilities. In addition, Israeli forces have arrested 2,576 Palestinians, shelled 3,669 residential buildings, uprooted 25,000 olive trees from Palestinian land, destroyed 3,669,000 m^2 of cultivated Palestinian land, demolished 116 Palestinian homes, and caused the unemployment rate to rise to 47% in the West bank and the Gaza Strip as a direct result of the blockade it has imposed on the Palestinians.[1]

That the international community continues to shy away from calling this a willful act of genocide, ethnic cleansing and apartheid, is both disheartening and worrisome. It is disheartening because it means that the Palestinian suffering will continue without any form of international intervention. And it is worrisome because where will Israel draw the lines? And will Israel's adamance to continue its

---

[1] These figures cover the period between September 28, 2000 and May 14, 2001. Source: The Palestinian Initiative for the Promotion of Global Dialogue and Democracy, Jerusalem, http://www.miftah.org/

occupation of the Palestinians and their land ultimately lead to a regional warfare that could potentially lead to world war? This notion may seem absurd to some, yet Israel's crazed obsession with maintaining control over most of the land it has occupied since 1967 means that that there is no limit to what it may attempt to keep its control, even if it means dragging the whole region and possibly the world into war.

It is time for the world to wake up. Real peace does remain possible but the chances for real peace are diminishing with the passage of each day. It is now the responsibility of world leaders who have a moral conscience to bring the plight of the Palestinians to an end, once and for all. It is also the moral responsibility of the scores of foreign journalists who are covering the current uprising to start telling the truth about what Israel is doing to the Palestinians, and it is the moral responsibility of their editors to print this truth. The shameful silence cannot continue.

When I permanently left Dheisheh on November 23, 2000, I did so convinced that one day, the refugees of the camps, wherever they are, will be the ones who will lead our people to our independence and liberation. I say this because the refugees of the camps are the ones who have suffered and sacrificed the most in the past 53 years of dispossession. Yet they continue to be the least understood and least appreciated segment of Palestinian society. I hope that this book will help understand them better. I also hope that it will make it clear why the Oslo Peace Accord, signed between Israel and the Palestinians in September 1993, failed miserably and eventually led to its only natural result – another Palestinian uprising in a long and painful, yet unyielding, struggle for independence and statehood.

Muna Hamzeh
Austin, Texas, USA
May 2001

PART ONE

1 Ordinary Days in Dheisheh (2000)

Wednesday, October 4, 2000

Dear Diary,

The numbness I've been feeling for the past six days continues. I can't seem to be able to sleep much these days, and so when I got up at dawn this morning, I tried to convince myself not to turn on the computer or radio and just go up on the roof and have my coffee. I feel like I'm going crazy.

But without even thinking, I made coffee, turned on the radio to the local Bethlehem 2000 station and started downloading 352 new emails in my inbox. I feel so numb. About a dozen letters of solidarity arrived from teenagers in Burj el-Shemali[1] Refugee Camp in south Lebanon. I'm printing them out and faxing them to the local Bethlehem TV station and to local journalists in Gaza and Ramallah. It is important for Palestinians here to know what Palestinians in the Diaspora are saying and doing, and about all the demonstrations taking place in Europe, the U.S. and Canada. And vice versa of course. Reports and photos about the massacre being committed against the Palestinians here need to reach people in Lebanon, France, the United States, England and Canada. After a few hours of reading emails, forwarding, translating, faxing, calling Gaza and Ramallah for news, I start feeling the pain in my stomach. To escape, as if there is an escape, I turn on the TV and watch live coverage on the Palestine Satellite station and the local Bethlehem TV stations. Israeli soldiers are massacring our people. Meanwhile, the international community is watching in silence! When will this injustice end?

If Mohammed al-Durra[2] was a 12-year-old Israeli boy and we had killed him in cold blood, U.S. president Clinton would have

---

[1] Burj el-Shemali camp is located east of Tyre in south Lebanon. It was set up after the 1948 Arab–Israeli War for Palestinian refugees from Hawla and Tiberias in northern Palestine. It is one of twelve Palestinian refugee camps in Lebanon (source: UNRWA website: http://www.un.org/unrwa/).

[2] Images of a terrified Mohammed and his father crouching behind a concrete wall near Netzarim junction in the Gaza Strip shook the world on October 1, 2000. For 45 minutes, Muhammad's father tried in vain to shield him from

3

screamed to the high heavens that we are terrorists. How can the world we live in be so unjust? When will this nightmare we've been living in for the past 52 years come to an end?

Nobody in Dheisheh is able to go to work except those who work in Bethlehem.[3] Life has come to a standstill. Each "Zone A"[4] area is sealed off, with Israeli Merkava tanks, from other areas. We can't get from Bethlehem to Hebron in the south, or to Jerusalem in the north. All we can spend our days doing is to follow the news closely. Everyone's eyes here are glued to their TV set every waking hour of the day, nothing else.

I went and watched TV with my neighbors yesterday. Nobody wants the clashes to end. Everyone here wants an all-out confrontation with the Israeli military and to hell with it. There is so much desperation and people are under so much pressure that they feel this is it this time: it is either us or them; it is either the end of Israel's occupation of us or our death, and if the Israelis are going to bomb us and level us to the ground, then so be it. "One bomb will do it for Dheisheh," remarks Muyasar, my 34-year-old neighbor and mother of six.

"We'll all die instantly," I reply.

"Dying is better than going on the way we have been," she laments.

Every woman I talk to here says the same. The mood is so different this time. People are just fed up with Israel's aggression. They are fed up with the Palestinian Authority's corruption; with the shameful so-called peace agreements that have turned this place into an apartheid state, a Bantustan, a West Bank divided into 200 isolated islands. People are fed up with a silent world that doesn't give a damn about us just because we are Arabs. I grab Marianna, Muyasar's

---

gunfire. The whole scene was caught on camera by a France 2 cameraman, and the footage shows the boy's father waving desperately to Israeli troops, shouting: "Don't shoot." But the terrified boy is hit by four Israeli bullets. The footage shows him collapsing, dead, in his father's arms (source: news reports).

[3] The District of Bethlehem is 605 sq km, and includes the major municipalities of Bethlehem, Beit Jala, and Beit Sahour, 65 Palestinian towns and villages, the three refugee camps of Aida, Dheisheh and Beit Jebren, and 27 Israeli settlements (source: The Applied Research Institute), Jerusalem.

[4] Since the Cairo Agreement in 1995, the West Bank has been divided into three zones: A, B, and C. Zone A is under full Palestinian control, and is made up of the big towns only. Zone B is under Palestinian civil control and Israeli security control. Zone C is under full Israeli control and includes the majority of the West Bank.

adorable 2-year-old daughter, and hold her tight to my chest. I adore the kid and love to play with her every day.

"I'm crazy about you auntie Muna," she giggles as she kisses me and wraps her tiny arms around my neck.

I take a deep breath, sniffing her sweet soapy scent. She, her sisters and brother are the only thing that has kept me sane these past few days. Don't they deserve a better future? A future with political and civil rights! Don't they deserve a decent education, a life without turmoil, a life outside the damn "Zone A" we are cooped up inside? Or don't Palestinian kids count in today's world! Are we less human? The women here are angry at the scenes on the TV showing Israeli troops evacuating Israeli settlers from the settlement of Nitsarim in Gaza under the cover of the night. "Who will evacuate our women, children and men?" snaps Marianna's grandmother, Um Ra'ed.

As we sat there drinking tea with sage and sharing our sadness and depression, Marianna's father came home with guests for the night: a man, his very pregnant wife, and their 2-year-old daughter. Their house is in the midst of the exchange of gunfire in the nearby town of Beit Sahour. The wife and girl were in such a state of hysterics that they refused to sleep in the house another night. So they came to Dheisheh for the night. I looked at the woman, who expects to deliver her baby any day now, and tried so hard to hold back the tears as she complained of the pain in her belly. She was a nervous wreck. Isn't she human? Doesn't she deserve to have someone evacuate her?

I took Marianna's oldest sister, Malak, and walked down to the store for some groceries. The clashes started at the end of the month and none of us here has received our September salaries yet. So we buy on credit and borrow some shekels[5] here and there from each other. It's funny how we live. None of us has enough money for a donkey ride out of this place, let alone for a plane ticket. Perhaps this is why the anger at the affluent Palestinian leadership. There sure is money in this country, but only in the hands of the few. The rest live month by month and put their fate in the hands of God!

At the store, the volume of the TV was turned up loud. Reports were coming in about the bombardment of residential neighborhoods in Rafah and Gaza. All eyes were watching. "You're becoming a bad salesman," I tease Yakoub, the shopkeeper.

"Why is that?" he asks surprised.

---

[5] Israeli currency.

"Where are the M16s and hand grenades on your shelf? Don't you want to order any and sell them to us?" I say jokingly.

Everyone in the store laughed and started making remarks.

"Stones don't do it anymore. Guns are the answer. That's the only language the Israelis understand," someone remarks.

We know, of course, that M16s won't stand a chance in front of LAW missiles or Apache fighter helicopters, but we are desperate here. No one even thinks about death. We only think about an end to Israel's aggression against us. It is either them or us. There is no third way. The occupation simply has to end.

I called Gaza last night. Friends in Rafah, Khan Younis and Gaza City are holding up. Everyone is determined to go on and they don't want Arafat to meet with Barak.[6] No one wants that. People are very pleased with the mass demonstrations in so many Arab countries: Abu Dabi, Cairo, Beirut, Sana', Damascus, Amman.

People here keep saying that if we hold on till Friday, when the imams of all the mosques in the Arab countries are bound to tell their masses something significant, then we may gain something out of this. We just have to hold on till next Friday and see what will happen in the Arab countries.

And Friday is only two days away and there doesn't seem to be an end in sight to Israel's bombardment of civilians. And the clashes are still going on everywhere. The sound of the ambulance sirens going by on the main road has become a part of the daily sounds we hear in Dheisheh. Sometimes at night we hear the sound of gunfire, mostly coming from the town of Beit Jala[7] nearby.

---

[6] Palestinian leader, Yasser Arafat, and Israeli Prime Minister, Ehud Barak, held a trilateral meeting in Paris on October 4 with U.S. Secretary of State Madeleine Albright. Although it was announced that Israel and the Palestinians had reached a verbal agreement whereby both sides would order an end to the violence, Barak and Arafat failed to reach a written agreement (source: news reports).

[7] Beit Jala is a growing Palestinian agricultural town (whose name in Aramaic means "grass carpet") spreading over an area of 14,000 dunums (dunum = 0.1 hectare). It is located five kilometers south of Jerusalem. It lies on the slope of a hill covered with olive trees, vineyards and apricots. Beit Jala is reputed for its master stone-masons. Sharafat and Beit Safafa villages lie north of this historic town, Bethlehem to the east where the Jerusalem–Hebron road is considered the town's eastern border line, El Khader village to the south, and Battir village to the west. From 1940 until the beginning of the Israeli Occupation in 1967, Beit Jala was a beautiful summer resort frequented by tourists because of its good weather, attractive scenery, and its location on top of a mountain (930 m.) overlooking Jerusalem, Bethlehem and other places.

Meanwhile in Israel life goes on as normal. The Israelis get up every morning and go to work, while their kids go to school. They go to their restaurants and movie theaters; they are not affected by all of this. It is as if their husbands, fathers and sons who are killing, wounding, and maiming us are some mercenary soldiers from a far-away land. There is no public outcry in Israel. There are no demands to bring the aggression to an end. Israel has simply become comfortable in being a racist apartheid state!

Ziad Fararjeh, 20, from Dheisheh, lost his eye and everyone is waiting for him to return from the orthopedic hospital in Jerusalem so that they can visit him. A rubber-coated metal bullet struck Ziad's eye during clashes in Bethlehem a few days ago. His eyeball fell in the palm of his hand and his friends say he kept holding it till he reached the hospital. He thought they could put it back in – the poor kid – and so good-looking too. He's going to be blind in one eye for ever. But Ziad isn't Moshe or Uri. He doesn't matter and doesn't count.

It is almost 6:40 a.m. Soon the local TV stations will start broadcasting live coverage of clashes in different areas. The local stations in Bethlehem and Palestine TV are the best, giving us live reports all the time, revolutionary songs, and archive footage from the first Intifada. We wake up and sleep to the same every day. There is no escape from it. We can't turn off the TV sets. We all want to know what is happening minute by minute. And we all have this vision that the Arab masses will march into Palestine and join us in our fight for liberation. We don't want a repeat of Lebanon '82, when the Arab world merely watched civilians get butchered during Israel's invasion and did nothing except cry about it. So we keep hoping that the Arab masses will wake up from their deep slumber and come to our rescue.

We have to keep the faith that maybe, just maybe, this time around things will be different and that 52 years of Israel's brutality against our people will see an eternal end. Perhaps then Palestine would be such a beautiful and wonderful place to live in. We all know it can be.

After its occupation of the West Bank in June 1967, Israel shred Beit Jala's agricultural infrastructure into segments. So far, three Israeli settlements called Gilo, Har Gilo, and Giv'at Hamatos have been created on Beit Jala's cultivated land. Two tunnels and two by-pass roads were also constructed on the town's confiscated land (source: The Applied Research Institute, http://www.arij.org/ ~arij/paleye/beitjala/ index.htm).

The good news is that the official Palestinian Satellite TV station and the local stations reported last night that the Fatah Movement has issued a leaflet calling on Arafat not to meet with Barak in Paris and asking the Palestinians not to surrender, urging them to stand up in the face of Israel's continued aggression.

This means that there is no intention to stop the struggle.

God only knows what today will bring.

*   *   *

Thursday, October 5, 2000

Dear Diary,

The electricity went out in the Bethlehem area between 7:00 p.m. and 11:00 p.m. last night. Soon we found out that the Israeli army had shelled an electric generator in Bethlehem. The Palestinian Authority asked the Israelis not to shoot at Palestinian fire fighters so they could go in and put out the flames, which engulfed the generator. The Israelis refused, of course!

How the electricity came back on at 11:00 p.m., we don't know. But it looks like the electricity just went out again in parts of Bethlehem this morning because both the radio and TV, which were both turned on, just went silent.

The blackout seemed to confirm the sense of deep depression we've all been feeling since it was announced that Arafat was meeting with Barak in Paris. So many of us could have bet that Arafat wouldn't do it. Nobody here wants him to.

And now the morning brings with it this heavy cloud of gloom. The revolutionary songs and the sounds of the sirens outside, and the reports about the clashes yesterday and last night, which resulted in seven additional deaths, aren't sounds that anger us. Rather they are sounds and reports that push us forward, that make our blood boil, allowing us to feel angry enough to survive through another day.

But reports of an agreement between Arafat and Barak aren't what we want to hear. So what if Israel pulls back its heavy artillery? They will still use live ammunition, rubber bullets and tear gas to kill innocent civilians. We will still wake up the next day in the apartheid-state we live in; the Israeli settlements built on our land will still be there, and the checkpoints will still be there. And that's why the adamance this time around to see matters through. No one wants to go back to the situation as it was prior to al-Aqsa Intifada. Everyone is simply too fed up with Israel's occupation, its unwillingness to return to us the land it occupied in 1967, and its feeble attempts to sign one defunct agreement after the other with the Palestinian Authority; all agreements that fail to give us our full political and human rights.

As hard as these past few days have been, with a week feeling more like an entire decade, people here are amazingly determined to fight till the end. How can this momentum be allowed to subside? We have been putting up with the results of the Oslo Peace Accord for seven years now, and these results have done nothing more than reinforce Israel's apartheid rule over us. It is enough. We want an honorable peace this time.

And so it was that I half-heartedly turned on the radio and TV this morning, thinking that all the stations would be talking about an agreement reached between Barak and Arafat in Paris. But surprise! Oh sweet, lovely precious, wonderful and energizing surprise! Listening to the broadcasts you wouldn't think anything happened in Paris last night. Interviews with various Fatah, Hamas and other activists indicate that the battle is still alive. Everyone interviewed is talking about the massacre against the Palestinians and that the fight hasn't seen an end yet.

Our refugee camp is so quiet this morning. There is little movement outside. I went out on the streets with a BBC reporter yesterday afternoon and it was so calm. A few kids in my alley were playing a war game; throwing pebbles at each other and firing toy guns. A few other kids were playing soccer with a flat soccer ball. Poor kids! The loud volume of radios and TVs emanated from the open windows and blended in with the smell of fried tomatoes, boiled rice and fresh baked bread; the sweet smells that give the camp such a safe, homey feeling. This is a feeling I've always loved about Dheisheh. It is the feeling that we are all one big family.

The high volume of the radio and TV startled me just now. So the electricity is back on in Bethlehem! The radio announcer is reporting that the Palestinian Authority has just released eleven Hamas political prisoners from its jails. What about the rest of the political prisoners, I wonder? Eleven doesn't sound like the correct number of all the political prisoners who are being held, without trial, in Palestinian jails!

Another correspondent is filing his report about the clashes and demonstrations in Bethlehem. I type as he speaks:

Last night in Bethlehem, there were intense clashes in the Rachel Tomb area.[8] A heavy exchange of gunfire was reported. Israeli bullets penetrated Palestinian homes and heavily damaged the top floor of the Paradise Hotel near Rachel's Tomb. Four Israeli soldiers were wounded and an army chopper evacuated them to Hadassah Hospital in West Jerusalem. An American tourist was injured from Israeli gunfire near the Tantur Ecumenical Institute, adjacent to Bethlehem's northern entrance. He is reported to be in a critical condition.

Also last night in Beit Sahour, an exchange of gunfire lasted for nearly one and a half hours. Three Israeli soldiers were wounded. Meanwhile, at the Beit Jala Tunnel,[9] Palestinians fired shots at an Israeli bus, wounding the driver.

In the village of Husan, south of Bethlehem, severe confrontations were reported. Two Palestinians were wounded by live ammunition: one shot in the chest, the other in the leg.

Armed Palestinians fired shots at the Israeli settlement of Bitar Ilit,[10] southwest of Bethlehem. Afterwards, Israeli settlers took to the streets and started pelting Palestinians with stones. Soldiers stormed into the village at night and brutalized the residents.

---

[8] Situated on the Jerusalem–Hebron road near Bethlehem's northern entrance, this small building marks the traditional Tomb of Rachel, Jacob's wife. Although considered holy to Christians, Muslims and Jews, the Israeli military authorities have made it off-limits to Palestinians and have turned the site into a fortified and permanent military point, used by Israeli soldiers and snipers to fire at Palestinian demonstrators.

[9] The Beit Jala Tunnel is part of By-pass Road 60. This road is part of an Israeli scheme to tear Beit Jala into fragments, and connect the settlements in the southern part of the West Bank (Gush Etzion Bloc) with settlements in the north. Road 60 slices up two mountains and rambles all over the cultivated lands of Beit Jala, cutting down hundreds of olive and vine trees, and confiscating more than 777 dunums of the town's land. Another segment of Road 60 was constructed on 4,800 dunums of land to the west of Beit Jala. It starts from the intersection which leads to the settlement of Har Gilo, all the way to Battir village where it meets with By-pass Road 4, passing through the southern parts of Hebron towards Jerusalem (source: The Applied Research Institute, http://www.arij.org/~arij/paleye/beitjala/index.htm).

[10] The settlement of Bitar Ilit was established in 1990, and is built on confiscated Palestinian land that belongs to villagers in the nearby village of Nahalin, located 20 kilometers southwest of Bethlehem. Today, the village of Nahalin is encircled by Israeli settlements, all built on confiscated Palestinian land (source: The Applied Research Institute: http://www.arij.org/).

Armed Palestinians also fired shots at an Israeli military target in the village of al-Khader,[11] south of Dheisheh.

Two Israeli military tanks are now situated at Rachel's Tomb. High-velocity Israeli guns are ready to fire in al-Khader, Beit Sahour, Rachel's Tomb, the Beit Jala Tunnel, and near the Israeli settlement of Efrat.

Palestinian demonstrator set the car of an Israeli settler on fire in the village of Husan. Israeli snipers are now ready to shoot demonstrators in Bethlehem because several soldiers have already been injured during clashes in Bethlehem and Beit Sahour. One soldier was killed in Beit Sahour. So the Israelis are now out for revenge in Bethlehem. They're planning something for Bethlehem.

One Palestinian was killed in Hebron yesterday at one o'clock in the morning, when an Israeli under-cover unit, attempting to enter the Palestinian-controlled territories, fired at Palestinians and their homes. An exchange of gunfire was also reported near the villages of Halhoul and Yata, south of Hebron.

All this was from Radio Bethlehem 2000. I switch to the official Palestine Radio station. The reporter is saying:

There is another martyr this morning in Jericho. He died from wounds he sustained the day before yesterday. There is a total of seven martyrs in the West Bank, the Gaza Strip, and inside the Green Line since yesterday morning. Apache helicopters fired at demonstrators at the Nitsarim junction in Gaza. LAW missiles were also fired.

In Nablus this morning thousands of marchers are participating in the march organized by the Palestinian Women's Union. Activists urged the marchers to march toward the nearest Israeli

[11] Al-Khader lies eight kilometers south of Bethlehem, with a population of 6,800. The original area of the village was 22,000 dunums (1 dunum = 1/10 hectare), but, since 1967, 55% of this area has been confiscated by the Israeli authorities to build more illegal settlements and construct by-pass roads. Al-Khader is bordered by the Gush Etzion block of settlements. Around 50% of Gush Etzion block is built on land originally belonging to the village. This includes Efrat, El'Azar, 'Atzion, Neve Danial, and the new settlement Tel Hazaiet. Through the recent expansion of settlements and by-pass roads, and the restriction and confiscation of Palestinian land, the Israeli authorities have violated the Wye River Peace Agreement (1998). The confiscation of al-Khader land for the enlargement of Road 60 is thus illegal (source: The Applied Research Institute: http://www.arij.org/~arij/paleye/wye/alk.htm).

military checkpoints. The marchers are chanting: "Abu Ammar (Arafat), Mr. President, come home from Paris."

Oh yes! Our people are coming through, they're holding on, they're moving forward. No one wants agreements for a ceasefire. Ceasefires are reached between fighting armies, and we are not an army. We are civilians who are fed up with Israel's occupation of our land. We want to continue with the fight to the end.

Thank God! I'm no longer depressed. The sun will shine today after all. We're back to where we were, standing up, fighting back and making our voices heard.

Oh sweet smell of victory, could you be ours someday soon? Do a people deserve it more than we do? It has been too long. Fifty-two years of aggression, of suffering, of sacrifice, of martyrs, of a life in the Diaspora. It is too long!

Perhaps this will be our last battle and our last war with the Israelis. It is either our death or our liberation. There is no third way. We don't want a third way.

*   *   *

Friday, October 6, 2000

Dear Diary,

Rise sunshine rise. Rise and warm my cold heart. Warm it for my tears. Let my tears roll down and wet my dry cheeks.

Everyone slumbers into a restless sleep. But I am awake and so are the birds on the trees. Oh, I envy them so! They fly from a phone line to a TV antenna free from knowing about the sadness that wrings a human heart. They don't comprehend pain or the spilling of precious human blood. They don't understand what it means to have vivid dreams of a better life and endlessly chase after these dreams like chasing after a mirage.

Cry my eyes, cry! The tears may just wash the pain down to a puddle around my feet. How are any of us going to face Um Hazem today? Oh, Um Hazem, your son Mustafa joined the long procession of Palestinian martyrs. Your son is dead and we are all expected to tell you that it is all right, that he is a martyr who's going directly to the heavens. We are supposed to comfort you by asking you to be strong for your blind husband, Um Hazem. We are supposed to ask you to be strong for your other sons. We are supposed to tell you that you should rejoice that your son was Dheisheh's first martyr in al-Aqsa Intifada. But how can you rejoice Um Hazem, when your youngest child is dead?

Oh, the pain in a mother's heart. Oh, the agonizing pain in a mother's heart when she finds out that her youngest son has just been blasted away by watching him, on her TV screen, stretched on a hospital bed. Oh, the horrible agony of finding out this way. Israeli bullets charred Mustafa's chest and arm, Um Hazem! Over and over and over again, they kept showing us a close-up of his spent body as it lay on the hospital bed. We could see all the way through to the bones in his arm, Um Hazem! And so could you. Four sniper bullets riddled his body as he stood there by the side of the road with his best friend Akram.

Cry my eyes, cry! Maybe the tears will keep me sane, or maybe insane. I'm not sure I can tell the difference anymore. Daylight turns into darkness, and then it is daylight again. What month is it? What's the day of the year? Which decade is it? Which century is it? Does it matter anymore?

I'm so afraid Akram will die too. Oh Akram! Just the other day you passed me by on the street. Remember all the times we had meals together at your house, all our laughter, all your beautiful sketches, and your promising future as a budding young artist? Oh Akram! Please don't die. So what if they operated on you last night, removed your damaged spleen, and operated on your leg and kidney? You can live without your spleen. We'll all take care of you and make sure you can live without it. Just don't die.

Who will call your sister, Tagrid, in Gaza and tell her that you were shot last night? Who is going to pick up the phone and convey the news to her and her husband, your cousin Zaher? They will go crazy because they can't leave Gaza and come visit you at your hospital bed. Did you forget, Akram? This is what their peace means. That Tagrid can't drive the one-hour-away distance to be by your side.

And your mother, Akram! Oh, your poor dear mother. Who will tenderly hold Um Ali's heart and caress away her sorrow and pain? A son shot and hospitalized; and a daughter in Gaza who could very well be living on the moon.

This is the "peace process" they want to force down our swollen throats Akram. This is the "Oslo," the "peace accord," the "negotiations process" that they want to convince the world they want us to have.

Peace my foot, and I wish I could use a more graphic word! This is a "war process," a "live ammunition accord," an "eradicate-the-Palestinians Oslo," an "Apache Chopper Accord!"

And only last night Akram, sometime in the early evening, I forced myself to turn off the computer after being at it since 3 a.m. I felt like I was about to lose my eyesight and I forced myself to take a break. I threw my aching bones on the couch in front of the TV and started switching channels to watch the news. Then I saw the "Batman" movie starting on one of the satellite channels. This is just what I need, I told myself, a respite from reality for an hour and a half of Michelle Pfeiffer. Stupid me didn't realize that respites aren't for people like us.

Was it five minutes later, or only four when the phone rang? I don't remember. Someone from Bethlehem was asking me if I knew Dheisheh's martyr, Mustafa Mahmoud Fararjeh. "What?" I screamed into the mouthpiece, "What martyr?"

"Aren't you watching the news?" the guy on the other end asked me. No! I was watching stupid Batman. I was trying to lose myself in a fantasy world when reality was close, so very close!

Hundreds of people from Dheisheh, my husband included, walked down the road in the dark to join the march to Mustafa's house across the street in the town of Doha. The Fararjeh family, originally from Zakariya, is the largest family in Dheisheh. My 2-year-old neighbor Marianna is a Fararjeh. Remember Marianna and her sweet soapy smell? She's related to Mustafa. And while he lived with his parents in Doha across the street from the camp, his brothers, uncles, and other relatives all live in the camp. When the marchers left the camp, I couldn't sit still. I felt like I was on the verge of a nervous breakdown and I had to do something to vent my anger and my sadness. And so I cleaned the entire house and then with a hose and broom in hand, I went up on the roof to wash it clean. Imagine that! I needed to do something physical. I badly needed to reduce the tension that was eating me alive. When my husband came home, he couldn't believe I was cleaning.

"Are you nuts? What are you doing? You are too exhausted to do all this work," he said. "But I am trying to hold on to sanity," I told him.

Throughout the night, we heard the sporadic sound of gunfire. It was pitch dark outside and the quietness in Dheisheh resembled the old days of curfews. Nothing stirred! Then Bethlehem TV broadcast news about an Israeli invasion into the village of Harmallah, east of Bethlehem. As the Israeli army lit Harmallah's sky, the soldiers stormed the village accompanied by two tanks and heavy gunfire. At the same time, the army was asking, in Hebrew and through loudspeakers, residents of a nearby settlement not to go to Jerusalem on Friday (today). Palestinians living in the proximity of the settlement of Gilo[12] heard the army telling the settlers to hide inside their shelters.

Frightening warnings. What do the Israelis have in store for us today? More hell, what else!

After the noon prayer today, Mustafa's funeral procession will be on its way. Where will they bury him? The Muslim cemetery in Bethlehem is adjacent to Rachel's Tomb, where the Israeli soldiers, tanks, undercover units and snipers are situated. Will they bury him in the village of Artas near Dheisheh as they had buried so many martyrs in Dheisheh during the first Intifada? Will there be more martyrs from Dheisheh today?

Mothers brace yourselves! The "war process" isn't done with your sons yet. But fret not; your sons are only Palestinians, Arabs, Muslims and Christians. Their blood can be spilled for the world to watch, cry and do nothing. They can die so that governments around the world can issue empty and meaningless statements. The numbness we feel has stifled our fear of death. There is no turning back this time around. And to everyone's content, Arafat is back in Gaza without signing an agreement with Barak in Paris. So come on Apache helicopters and LAW missiles, our bodies are waiting.

My neighbor Muyasar told me yesterday, "Don't fear death Muna. We don't die twice but only once. Dying once is better than going back to the situation we were in before al-Aqsa Intifada, when we were dying inside a million times over each day."

Do you hear that Um Hazem? From now on, Mustafa will no longer die a million times over. Do you hear me Um Hazem? From

---

[12] The settlement of Gilo was constructed in 1970 on confiscated land belonging to the towns of Beit Jala and Beit Safafa. The present population of Gilo exceeds 30,000. Gilo was greatly expanded in the southern and western direction, creeping on more Beit Jala land (source: The Applied Research Institute: http://www.arij.org/~arij/paleye/beitjala/index.htm).

now on, only those of us alive will die a million times over each day. Do you hear me?

*   *   *

Saturday, October 7, 2000

Dear Diary,

I don't know what came over me this morning! For some reason, I couldn't stop crying. I could hardly see the cups and plates as I stood at the sink to wash them. Tears just kept blocking my vision. I started to slowly bang my head against the cupboard and ask myself, what is wrong with me? What is wrong with me?

Was I crying because I was planning to go visit Akram in the hospital today? Was I afraid of what I would see? Or was I crying because of the bad dream I had last night about a close friend in Gaza who, in the dream, was being shot? Or did the events of this past week finally catch up with me and force me to lose my cool? Maybe it was all these reasons combined. But the tears just wouldn't stop. Unable to sit at the computer and write, I started to viciously scrub everything in sight: the cupboards, chairs, and floor – just everything in sight.

Two hours later, I was physically exhausted and then the damn daily headache was back to bother me some more. I tried to sleep but couldn't. Sooner or later, no matter what I did, I had to go see Akram in the hospital.

And so I went with my friends Manal, Hanan and Amal. We walked up to the third floor, to the intensive care unit at al-Hussein Government Hospital in Beit Jala. As we approached the door, I spotted Abdullah, Akram's cousin. I wanted to cry but didn't. Abdullah looked exhausted as he stood there greeting everyone who came to visit Akram.

"You can go in only two at a time, and please, you're not allowed to speak to him," he said faintly.

Hanan and Amal went in first and came back out five seconds later. Hanan murmured something about not being able to handle it.

Then Manal and I walked in. It was a long hall and Akram's bed was at the very far end. A screen blocked him from our view as we approached. I felt my heart sink as he came into full view. Tubes extended from his mouth and nose and he wasn't awake. His right leg was in a cast and a sheet covered his body, all the way up to his bare chest. Small spots of perspiration filled his forehead. My lips began to quiver and so did Manal's. All we could do was to murmur, poor Akram! His body had endured three surgeries, one after the other, and all in one evening. One bullet had damaged his kidney but a quick operation was able to save it. Another bullet had totally destroyed his spleen, and he was operated on to remove it. The third operation was to save his badly hit leg. According to the doctors, if Akram had arrived at hospital five minutes later than he did, he would have died of excessive internal bleeding. He lost so much blood.

Manal and I lingered at the foot of his bed, neither of us wanting to leave. Then suddenly, Akram opened one eye and looked straight at me. I waved and whispered hello. He nodded and closed his eye again. We left him feeling so disheartened.

Next we went to al-Manama Hospital near Dheisheh to visit Nasser, another friend in Dheisheh who had a serious operation on his spinal cord. A medical lab technician, and father of two, Nasser was hurt during the gunfire exchange in Beit Sahour on Thursday, October 5, only a few hours after Mustafa and Akram were shot. Though he had gone through serious surgery for four hours, Nasser was in very good spirits and very happy to see us.

Nasser told us what happened, "This friend and I climbed up on the roof of a building to watch the exchange of gunfire. Within seconds, the Israeli army fired heavy high-velocity machine-gun fire in our direction. Instead of jumping off the roof from the direction I had climbed, I jumped from the opposite direction. I kept thinking 'I'll reach the ground now, I'll reach the ground now,' but the distance was farther than I expected on that side of the building. I fell from a distance of seven meters and landed on my feet and started running. When we reached safety, my leg started going numb and I started screaming from the pain. Apparently, I had hurt the nerve in my spinal cord and they decided to operate on me right away so that I wouldn't become paralyzed. My friends insisted on bringing a video camera and filming the entire operation."

Nasser laughed, started wiggling his toes, and said: "I'm OK now and I'm not going to be paralyzed."

We were planning to go to Mustafa's house, to extend our con-dolences to his family, but visiting Akram and Nasser left us so emotionally drained that we decided to postpone the visit till tomorrow. Instead, we opted to go to Manal's house for coffee. All we could do was talk about the situation. Nobody wants the situation to calm down if the Palestinians don't get any political gains, but no one is optimistic that they are going to.

As we sat there talking about the events of the past week, the TV announcer interrupted his news broadcast to report a news flash: Hizbullah fighters just kidnapped three Israeli soldiers, with their tank, in Shab'aa farms in southern Lebanon. We all cheered! We had earlier heard the news about the two Palestinian refugees in Lebanon who were shot dead by Israeli troops during a demonstration at the Lebanese border and we were so proud of Hizbullah for responding so quickly. The newscaster went on to say that Israel was threatening to bomb Beirut and Damascus. The Lebanese government responded to the Israeli threats by demanding that Israel release all Lebanese prisoners from its jails.

The events seem to have suddenly taken a different twist. Are we heading toward a regional war? It all depends on how Syria and Lebanon will respond if Israel bombs them. No one here really expects Israel to bomb Beirut and Damascus. But if Israel were to do so, we know that the impotent Arab regimes will do nothing. Anger at the impotence of the Arab regimes is immense here, as it is toward the U.S. and the United Nations, who are staying clear of a blunt condemnation of Israel.

By 7:30 p.m., my headache had gotten terribly worse and I decided to go to sleep. Fifteen minutes later, I was awakened by the sound of a very heavy exchange of gunfire. I lay in bed and listened. It sounded very close, at the Beit Jala Tunnel near the village of al-Khader, only some meters away from Dheisheh. The shooting persisted, on and off, for nearly 40 minutes or more. In between, I could hear the sound of long whistles and cheers coming from somewhere in Dheisheh. I smiled in the dark. I was a kid in Amman, Jordan during the 1967 war. I was also a kid during the Black September war in Jordan in 1970, and as an adult, I lived through most of the first Intifada, but this was the very first time in my life ever that the sound of gunfire didn't frighten me.

For the first time in my life I fully understood why the Palestinians who've lived under Israeli occupation all their lives, have always gone out and fought the Israelis, facing their bullets with stones. I guess when you've lived under oppression, brutality, and force for so long, fear becomes your least concern. Rather, you think of wanting an end to the atrocities, and Israel doesn't seem to understand any language if it isn't the language of force. Perhaps the Palestinians will learn from Hizbullah and from the Vietnamese just how to go about liberating our land from its foreign occupiers.

The shooting suddenly ceased. I couldn't sleep and realized that I hadn't eaten all day nor written my diary entry.

I checked on the kids next door. Khloud, Marianna's 11-year-old sister, was in hysterics. She doesn't sleep well at night and panics when she hears the sound of gunfire. She can't sleep if the lights aren't kept on in her bedroom. The events of the past week have certainly left their mark on the kids. The healing of the psychological scars that the kids have been left with after watching the cold-blooded murder of Muhammad al-Dura, will take a long time to heal. But then again, they will grow up knowing that they have to carry on the struggle, until the Palestinians are able to reach full independence.

*   *   *

Sunday, October 8, 2000

Dear Diary,

Everyone woke up talking about Hizbullah's operation in southern Lebanon and their capture of three Israeli soldiers. It was the first time in ten days that Palestinians here found something to smile about. So what if the operation forced Israel to go crazy, threatening to drag the entire area into regional warfare?

No one here is counting on the Arab regimes to take any action if Beirut or Damascus are bombed. If they wanted to take action, as so many people here in Dheisheh say, then they could have responded to Israel's on-going massacre of the Palestinians by closing all Israeli embassies, trade offices, or whatever they call them, in all the Arab capitals that have ties with Israel. They could have also stopped pumping oil to the West for one week, or one month, to pressure Western governments into taking stern action.

No one here counts on the Arab regimes, but they know, with their eyes closed, that they can count on Hizbullah to masterfully plan an operation and then carry it out. True, two Palestinian refugees in Lebanon had to die in order for the operation to succeed, but such is always the case when a people are fighting a war for freedom and liberation. Death and destruction have to pave the way.

The shooting death of Hasan Hassanein, 23, a Palestinian refugee from Shatila refugee camp and Shadi Anas from Burj al-Barajneh Refugee Camp,[13] led to the capture of the three soldiers and the rapid progress of events. By nightfall yesterday, Israeli tanks and artillery were suddenly directed toward Palestinian towns. An exchange of gunfire was heard in different parts of the West Bank and Gaza Strip. Israeli settlers went on a vicious rampage against Palestinians in the West Bank, Gaza and inside the Green Line. Barak was suddenly giving Arafat a 48-hour ultimatum to stop the Intifada.

But if Barak really wants to know whether or not the Intifada will stop, or can be stopped, he should talk to Palestinian women here, rather than direct his threats to the Palestinian leader. Has Barak wondered why Palestinian women are absent from the confrontation lines this time around? With a few exceptions here and there, and aside from partaking in the funeral processions of martyrs, the women are staying home. The obvious reason seems to be the fact that there are exchanges of gunfire, making it unsafe for the women to be present.

But the women are the unknown soldiers, the ones holding the fort in every Palestinian household. They're the ones calming their kids and tending to them while keeping their eyes glued on their TV screens. I don't know a single woman in Dheisheh who isn't closely following every single development. Even my 77-year-old mother-in-law sits in her room with the radio always close to her ear.

All the women talk about how they are unable to go about their everyday chores. They talk about how they are not in the mood to clean; how they have lost weight in the past ten days; how they suffer from headaches; how they can't sleep well at night; and how they are frightened for their husbands and their children.

What do these women have to say to Barak?

"This Intifada must continue," says my friend Intisar, a mother of nine. "The death of our people isn't going to be without results. Let every Palestinian household give one martyr and lets see this

[13] Hasan Hassanein and Shadi Anas were killed and 23 others were wounded on October 7, 2000 when Israeli soldiers opened fire at Palestinian refugees demonstrating at Ramieh, east of Naqoura at the Lebanese border. Nearly 500 demonstrators held up Palestinian flags and vowed to return home in a show of support for the ten-day-old Intifada in the Palestinian Territories. Israeli soldiers fired tear gas into the crowd, who responded by throwing stones. Israeli soldiers then opened fire (source: Mass Processions Honor Victims of Ramieh Clash, by Reem Haddad, *Daily Star*, October 9, 2000).

through to the end. News of a ceasefire agreement depresses us; it isn't what we want to hear. We can't have an Intifada every few years and then slumber into a deep sleep until we wake up again some years later to do it all over again. This time it has to be a fight till the end. Till we win."

Of course if Israel thinks it doesn't have a choice here, it certainly does. It isn't a complicated choice, but rather a choice that would bring an end to the confrontations now and forever. Israel can withdraw completely from the entire West Bank, Gaza Strip, and East Jerusalem – the territory it forcefully occupied in 1967. It can also dismantle all Israeli settlements in these territories. Then it can release all Palestinian political prisoners from jail, and recognize the right of return of Palestinian refugees. Once Israel grants the Palestinians their full political rights, it can enjoy the real fruits of peace resulting from the establishment of a truly independent Palestinian state, rather than the bantustan state it has been so eager to maintain by force.

But this choice is apparently still premature for Israel. It hasn't used the full potential of its military might against the Palestinians yet. Meanwhile, governments around the world have yet to put any pressure on the Jewish state. Can you imagine the U.S. and Britain bombing Tel Aviv like they've bombed Baghdad? Can you imagine sanctions against the government of Jerusalem? My, Oh my! Who would dare?

As Barak's 48-hour ultimatum descends on us tomorrow, the Fatah Movement has issued a leaflet today calling for the Intifada to continue. At 11:30 p.m. last night marchers walked through Dheisheh's alleys and then continued on to the main road adjacent to the camp. Churches in the Bethlehem area rang their bells in unison around noon and a sizable march called for by area churches marched through the streets. No one wants the Intifada to end.

With schools back in session today, busloads from area schools descended on Mustafa Farrarjeh's house to give their condolences to Um Hazem and her grieving family. Pre-school children wearing green headbands chanted as they walked up to Um Hazem and shook her hand. And tomorrow, all Dheisheh's families who originally come from the village of Zakariya – the same village that Mustafa Fararjeh came from – will come together and bring food to the martyr's house to feed all those present. This is the tradition in Palestinian society. For three days now, somebody has been bringing food to the family home. The first day, food was delivered by the

Palestinian Authority; the next day by the Islamic Waqf, and today by the Fatah Movement. A sense of solidarity fills the air. Of course, none of us is able to leave the Bethlehem area yet. For ten days, those of us who work in Ramallah, Jerusalem, Hebron, or Israel, have been sitting at home waiting, watching, and anticipating.

A general feeling persists. We all feel that this fight is our very last with the Israelis. After 52 years of resistance, dispossession and occupation, everyone is ready to either witness the total destruction of the land of Palestine, or the emergence of a fully independent Palestinian state. Which path we take is now Israel's choice.

* * *

Monday, October 9, 2000

Dear Diary,

I stared at the tomato for several minutes before finally biting my teeth into it. I didn't realize tomatoes were such a beautiful red and smelled so good too. Lately, I've been looking at everything as if I'm seeing it for the first time, and maybe for the last. The plants in my garden, 2-year-old Marianna's small mouth and rounded cheeks, though she's been looking pale these past few days, the five finches sitting on my terrace in a cage. With all this death around us, having a connection with living things seems to have taken on a sense of urgency. Yet most of the time, I feel so absent-minded. I don't feel like talking to anyone or cleaning anything. The laundry has been sitting in the washing machine for three days waiting to be hung on the lines to dry, but I don't care. I don't feel like doing anything except sitting at my computer sending and receiving emails and, in between, slumbering into a restless and broken sleep.

I feel sick to my stomach and I'm not alone. There is no escape, no outlet, and no change of atmosphere. Every day brings more of the same. We look like zombies over here. We are so wound up from watching so much blood on our TV screens, listening to the radio and waiting to see if Barak will bomb us to smithereens if we don't heed his call and bring the Intifada to an end. So many people around are stocking up on flour, sugar, cooking oil and other essentials. And we wait, wait, and wait.

But there has been no condemnation from Barak or the U.S., of course, for what the settlers are doing. Armed Israeli settlers have been on a violent rampage in the West Bank and inside the Green Line these past two days[14] and, yet, the radio and TV news are concentrating on diplomatic efforts, on a possible summit, on negotiating the exchange of prisoners between Israel and Lebanon. There is nothing about the violent attacks by settlers against Palestinians and their property.

"Stay in your homes at night. Don't go up on your roofs. Be careful, we are going to be showing some graphic photos, so don't let your kids watch," a local TV newscaster warns us. The local TV stations seem to be the only ones broadcasting anything about what the settlers are doing. Six Palestinians were killed in the past 48 hours, mostly by settlers.

And it was only last week that we awoke to the gruesome torture-to-death, by settlers, of Issam Hammad near Ramallah.[15] Hair-raising pictures of his mutilated body were all over the TV and the Internet.

---

[14] October 9: Israeli settlers continued their attacks on Palestinians within East Jerusalem, shooting live ammunition: rubber-coated steel bullets, and smashing cars and shops. Israeli settlers attacked Palestinian cars traveling along these roads, and in at least one incident, they've beaten passengers and sealed off the main roads from Tubas to Jenin and Nablus (source: Addameer human rights group: www.addameer.org/september2000).

October 8: Approximately 5,000 Jewish residents of Nazareth, under the protection of Israeli police, attacked Palestinian residents of Nazareth, shooting live ammunition and rubber-coated steel bullets. At least one Palestinian was killed, and several others were injured by live ammunition. Meanwhile, Israeli settlers from the Givat Ze'ev settlement in Jerusalem attacked Palestinian homes in the Jerusalem neighborhoods of Beit Hanina, Shufat and throughout East Jerusalem. Settlers fired live ammunition at Palestinian residents. In Kuful Harras and Qalqilya, Israeli settlers threw stones and fired shots at Palestinian cars. Settlers also burnt shops, trees, beat Palestinians and shot at houses in and around the village of Bidya, near Nablus. Fahed Baker, from Bidya, was shot with live ammunition in the head. An ambulance tried to reach him, but Israeli settlers shot at the ambulance and prevented entry into the area where he was injured along with four other Palestinians. Coordination to get another ambulance to the area took over an hour, by which time Fahed had bled to death. Electricity was cut off in the village of Salfit and other villages in the area, while Israeli settlers, and soldiers, attacked the villages. The villages were completely isolated from one another. In the village of Sourif, near Nablus, Israeli settlers entered the village and fired live ammunition at civilians. At least three Palestinians were in a critical condition. In Husan, near Bethlehem, Israeli settlers attacked the village, burned trees and shot at houses (source: Addameer human rights group: http://www.addameer.org/september2000/).

[15] October 9: In the village of Umm Safa near Ramallah, a Palestinian resident Issam Judeh Hammad, 40, left his house at 4:30 p.m. in his car. Eyewitnesses saw settlers in an Israeli military car follow him, stop his car and take him to an unknown location. In the morning his body was discovered on the side of a road near his house. He was taken to Ramallah Hospital where doctors

I downloaded them from the Internet and kept looking at them, over and over again. Where is the world media? Where is the international protection for the unarmed Palestinian population?

Isn't it interesting that since a ceasefire agreement between Israel and the PA was announced yesterday,[16] the Israeli army seems to have stepped back into the shadows and allowed the settlers to take over? The settlers have been shooting at Palestinian homes, smashing Palestinian cars, beating Palestinians and torturing them. This way, the Israeli military can claim to have heeded the ceasefire agreement, while giving the settlers a free rein to terrorize the Palestinians.

At 8:30 a.m., the phone rang. Hourieh, one of my best friends in Dheisheh, was a wreck. "I couldn't sleep a wink last night," she said. "My brother in Nablus called to say that the settlers attacked their house at night, smashing their bedroom window, where the children slept, with stones. They're so lucky the settlers didn't shoot them, they're so lucky," she said frantically.

Around 7 p.m., we could hear the sound of gunfire and we could sniff the suffocating smell of tear gas in the air. Settlers were attacking the village of al-Khader, a few meters south of Dheisheh. Heavy shooting at Palestinian homes was being reported and within seconds, we could hear the sound of ambulance sirens going by. A news flash on the TV screen informed us that the ambulances couldn't approach the homes of those injured because the shooting was so heavy. Then suddenly, we heard the sound of cars speeding by, honking their horns like crazy. Dheisheh's young men had gone to the rescue. Poor guys! What rescue? The settlers are committing acts of violence everywhere under the protection of the Israeli army, police, and border police!

I remember when I moved here from Washington, D.C. in the early years of the first Intifada. I was so unaccustomed to Israeli soldiers storming into our house, that every time they did it, I wanted to reach for the phone and dial 911. But calling the police

---

revealed that he had been severely tortured with both his arms and legs broken and his skull smashed with a sharp object. He had burns all over his body and his car was also found burnt, outside of the village. During the time of his disappearance the village was raided and attacked by settlers (source: Addameer human rights group: http://www.addameer.org/september2000/).
[16] U.S. president Bill Clinton succeeded in getting the Israel and Palestinian sides to agree ceasefire terms in the Egyptian resort of Sharm e-Sheikh on October 16, but the agreement never materialized on the ground (source: news reports).

for protection isn't something you can do here. There is no one to protect you. No law to defend you against the viciousness of Israeli brutality.

And now with the settlers taking over the role of Israeli soldiers to shoot and terrorize Palestinian civilians, the Palestinian security forces can't do anything to help. This is the Oslo peace process! It is what divided our West Bank into Zones A, B and C. The settlers are going on their rampages in villages located in Zone C, which is under total Israeli control. The Palestinian police aren't allowed into these areas, and cannot lift a finger to help civilians there. Welcome to peace!!

Indeed, the events of the past two days indicate just how smart Israel was in dividing the West Bank into these zones. We are surrounded you see. You can't get to Hebron without passing Israeli settlements; you can't get to Jerusalem without passing Israeli settlements; and you can't go to hell without passing Israeli settlements. They strategically surround each and every Palestinian town and city. Who will dare drive anywhere under these circumstances? Who will hear the screams of any Palestinian being tortured to death like Issam Hammad? Who for God's sake?

Silly me. I keep forgetting that there is freedom and liberty for all, but not for Palestine. There are condemnations from the world community, but not for Israel and the atrocities it continues to commit against us.

Where are you Anne Frank? Where are you? Is this what you died for? Did you die so that your people can turn around and commit these pogroms against another people? You were so young and didn't deserve to die; yet you died because of your identity. Our identity is the reason they're killing us now. It is our very existence that they are fighting. Oh Anne! I wish you could come back to life to take a look and tell me what you think! Tell me what you think of your people now.

How can we be expected to care about Barak's threats after all this? Are we supposed to shake in our boots if he threatens to spill more of our blood? We're not afraid. Do you hear me? The more that Israel and its military machine brutalize us, the more determined we are to become free. Aspiring for freedom is part of human nature Mr. Barak and Mr. Clinton.

Another day ends. We breathe, eat, and drink the scenes of blood and death. And the graphic photos on TV keep coming, driving us all to the point of insanity, or sanity. Is there a difference between the two anymore?

*   *   *

Tuesday, October 10, 2000

Dear Diary,

Little Marianna fell down the stairs and hurt herself today. The swollen lump on her lip makes her beautiful face look even smaller. She was asleep when I walked in, but when she awoke and saw me, she gave me one of her huge and adorable smiles. I held her in my arms and kissed her hands, her feet, her neck, and her hair.

When you are older Marianna, much older, and if I'm still around, I have to tell you how you, you and no one else, are the one who kept me together during al-Aqsa Intifada of September 2000. There were so many times when I sat outside in the rocking chair, trying desperately to find one positive reason to go on. The pain in my heart has been so heavy that I often feel so close to a heart attack. The sense of despair and gloom that grabs hold of my chest, and plunges deeper and deeper, makes me feel that I'm on the verge of losing my mind.

And then when it all becomes too much, just a tad too much, I come for you Marianna, and together we go up on the roof.

"Where's my baby chick?" You ask as you do each time.

"It is over there in the cage," I tell you as I always do.

"And what about your baby chick?" You ask as you always do.

"It died," I tell you as I always do.

"I want some candy," you blurt. And we go down to the kitchen to get some together.

"I took a bath auntie, did you?" You ask with that usual mischievous smile on your face.

And then you always cry when I tell you it is time for me to take you home. "I don't want to," you always say through your tears.

I love you Marianna. I love your going about your day, playing, eating, sleeping and not knowing what happens around you, not sensing your mother's fear for your life should things get worse, and not realizing just how much I need you each day just to go on, and just to survive the insanity around us.

Listening to Barak and other Israeli leaders making statements, you'd think we're the ones killing their children, Marianna. They're threatening to do all they can to protect their army and their citizens from our "violence," Marianna. Well, President Arafat, did you hear that? You'd better heed their call and put away your Apache Choppers and LAW missiles. You'd better disarm the children of Palestine before they shoot more Israeli soldiers with their stones.

Where are you, world, from this hypocrisy? This is the twenty-first century for goodness sake. This is the information age, the media age, the age of satellite and digital TV, the age of the Internet and mobile phones. Aren't we a global village? Hasn't the world been watching the ugly death of nearly 100 Palestinians and the wounding of nearly 3,000 in just twelve days, and so many of them school-age children. Our children!

And now Barak extends his ultimatum,[17] thus, extending his threats to us. If we don't stop the Intifada, he's going to. If we don't bring it to an end, he's going to. What are you going to do Barak? Bomb us some more? Re-occupy us? Deport us? Imprison us? Demolish our homes? What can you possibly do that previous Israeli leaders haven't already done to us during the past 52 years? What, for God's sake? Zap us? Oh, that's a new one!

Thirty-six people were wounded in the Palestinian territories today. And all it takes for the clashes to stop is for Israel to completely withdraw its military from the entire West Bank, Gaza Strip, and East Jerusalem; and realize that without agreeing to the establishment of a genuine Palestinian state in all the territories occupied in 1967, the struggle for liberation will never stop. Show me where in history did a people stop dreaming and grappling for independence and freedom? Show me now!

The peace of the brave, Mr. Israeli Prime Minister, is a peace that ends bloodshed, not calls for more. The peace of the brave is a peace that recognizes the legitimate rights of a people, rather than suppresses these rights. The peace of the brave, Mr. Barak, is a peace that brings an end to apartheid, not strengthens it.

If an Israeli state and a Palestinian state were to exist, side-by-side, Mr. Israeli Prime Minister, then everything in the region would

---

[17] Israeli Prime Minister, Ehud Barak, issued a 48-hour ultimatum to the Palestinians on October 7, 2000, giving Palestinian leader Yasser Arafat 48 hours to "put an end to the violence." Two days later, Barak came under attack by Likud leaders for his decision to put off his ultimatum (source: news reports).

naturally change for the better. If you were to admit that apartheid couldn't last, everything would change for the better. For twelve long days now, our normal everyday lives have come to a standstill. We're caught in a freeze-frame. No jobs we can go to because your tanks surround our cities. No going in or out of the zones you force us to live in. And then you want Arafat to stop the "violence." Do you actually believe your own words as you speak them Mr. Israeli Prime Minister? Do you now?

For the past twelve days, we've been watching the blood of Palestinian civilians getting spilled out on the streets. And where are the Arab leaders hiding? How come they all issued strong-worded statements following Hizbullah's kidnapping of three Israeli soldiers on October 7, and Israel's subsequent threats to bomb Beirut and Damascus? Where were you Arab leaders when Mohammed al-Dura was murdered in cold blood? Where were the Arab leaders when Israeli settlers stubbed their cigarettes in Issa Hammad's eyes, and more, so much more as the graphic pictures of his mutilated body show us?

Are you asleep now Marianna? I'm sure you are. Sweet dreams little girl. Yes there are green pastures in the world, and sandy beaches, and rainbows, and skies so blue. Do you see them in your dreams? I too see them in my dreams my sweet little darling. And I wish that when you're older, you'll see them for real. Here in Palestine where a people have been dreaming for longer than they care, wish, desire or want to remember that they've dreamed. Oh! Are you smiling in your sleep? Having a pleasant dream, are you? I know. I'm having one too! I am dreaming that you and I are free.

*   *   *

Wednesday, October 11, 2000

Dear Diary,

Today, I kept forgetting what day of the week it is. In the morning, I thought that today is Tuesday. In the afternoon, I couldn't believe that today is Thursday. Exactly two weeks after Ariel Sharon arrogantly challenged all Palestinian Muslims and walked into the grounds of the al-Aqsa Mosque in Jerusalem, he triggered yet another massacre of the Palestinian people.

Well Ariel, I'm sure you're gloating about the fact that your visit has resulted in nearly 100 Palestinian deaths and nearly 3,000 injuries, all in less than two weeks. I am sure you are gloating, just as you must have gloated in 1982 after the massacre of innocent Palestinian and Lebanese men, women, and children in the refugee camps of Sabra and Shatila in Lebanon.[18] You'd be ranting and raving if we had done this to your people. So where are you hiding now? Speak up! Why are you so silent? Has it really been 13 days since the start of this latest massacre? I have lost every sense of time. I know, yes, I know we are now just beginning to go in a state of shock, and to suffer from the psychological scars.

Um Ra'ed, Marianna's grandmother, refuses to change the channel whenever graphic scenes of the clashes are played over and over and over again on TV. She just sits there and stares at the screen, her face looking thinner and paler with the passage of each day. Terrible nightmares haunt her, and she is always worried about her three sons. She keeps seeing these dreams where lots of people are gathered to mourn someone! Today, she asked a friend to see her fortune in a cup of coffee, but her friend wouldn't tell her what she saw, insisting, instead, that reading the fortune in a coffee cup is just a bunch of nonsense. To divert her attention from her bad dreams, Um Ra'ed constantly complains of pain in her back, her arms, and her neck.

Marianna's mother, Muyasar, on the other hand, can't stop talking about the politics of the situation. The guys in the family tease her about it all the time. But I admire her so. Muyasar, the mother of six young children, who never has time to lift her head from all the cooking, washing, and cleaning, articulates her views so well, views none of us ever knew she had. As we gathered around

---

[18] The massacres at Sabra and Shatila occurred on September 16–18, 1982. The Falangists, an Israeli-allied Lebanese militia, were ordered by Sharon to mop up armed resistance in Palestinian refugee camps as Israeli forces stood guard. According to Israeli military intelligence, Falangist gunmen killed 700 to 800 civilians, but Palestinians sources estimate 2,000 dead. *New York Times* journalist Thomas Friedman saw "groups of young men in their twenties and thirties who had been lined up against walls, tied by their hands and feet, and then mowed down gangland style." Women, children and the elderly were also among those slain in the 62-hour assault. Although Sharon denied responsibility, an Israeli commission of inquiry ruled in February 1983 that he bore "indirect responsibility" for the massacres, harshly castigating him for his role. In 1985, a U.S. Military Law Review analysis argued that Sharon had "command responsibility" for the killings (source: Is Ariel Sharon Israel's Milosevic?, by James Ron, *Los Angeles Times*, February 5, 2001).

the succulent platter of stuffed grape-leaves she cooked yesterday, she kept going on and on about the willingness of U.N. Secretary General, Kofi Anan, to rush to Beirut to negotiate the release of the three Israeli soldiers kidnapped by Hizbullah on October 7.

"Three Israeli soldiers are captured and the whole world starts descending on Beirut Damascus to try to save the day. We've been getting massacred for nearly two weeks and no one gives a damn," she says passionately. Muyasar is also not pleased that U.S. president, Bill Clinton, is trying to arrange a summit meeting between Arafat and Barak. Like everyone else, Muyasar doesn't want Arafat to meet with Barak. I listened to Muyasar expressing her views eloquently and clearly. I wanted to give her a big hug and a kiss, but was too embarrassed to do so in front of the whole family, so I just squeezed her shoulder and smiled. Oh yes! And Muyasar just started to pray, for the first time ever. I guess everyone needs a way to cope.

I, on the other hand, need to find a way to concentrate on my work. Palestinian universities reopened two days ago, and even without being able to physically get to my office in Ramallah, I still have tons to do. But I can't concentrate. How are we, just like that, supposed to make a mental switch from the mode of devastation and depression, to the mode of tending to business and getting things done? It is as if we are expected to operate by remote control.

There is no rest and relaxation. There are no trauma therapists, no psychologists to talk to us about the scars, about how to cope with all the bloody scenes that have left their marks and continue to leave their marks on our psychological well-being. All we see is red blood, and more red blood, all the time.

I felt restless and depressed all day. I couldn't concentrate and kept walking away from the computer and sitting back down again. The radio announced the death of two more Palestinians today, one in Nablus and one in Gaza. Palestine TV was broadcasting live coverage of a huge march in Gaza. Commercial breaks were scenes from the clashes, the massacres, and a replay of Mohammed al-Durra's last moments of life, and the voice of his father, Jamal, screaming over and over again, "The boy is dead, the boy is dead!"

By 5 p.m., my depression started getting the better of me and I couldn't stop crying. I forced myself to get dressed and leave the house. I went next door and took Marianna and her eldest sister, Malak, for a walk. From a grocery store along the way, I bought Marianna a large pink balloon and tied it to her back.

"It is flying auntie, it is flying," she giggled as she tried to bounce it with her fist. An hour with her cleared the dark clouds and I was able to see the sun shining again.

But the moment I got home, the phone rang. It was my friend Hourieh, calling from her house a few blocks up the hill.

"The settlers have attacked my family's home in Nablus, Muna. My aunt and two of my brothers were hit in their heads from the flying stones. They've smashed their house and their cars. I'm scared. I'm so nervous. My stomach hurts. I'm sorry to bother you but I needed to talk to you about it."

"How did you find out?" I asked, trying to calm her down.

"I was watching the local news and they had these scenes from the funeral of a settler in the Nablus area who was run over by a Palestinian car. There were hundreds and hundreds of settlers and then they showed them attacking a Palestinian house on the main road. To my horror, I realized it was my family's house. So I called my brother, but he couldn't talk much because the situation was barely reaching its end. Israeli soldiers had apparently gone up on the roof of the house and started throwing tear gas at the angry settler mob as they stoned the house. Seeing the soldiers on the roof and thinking that the soldiers were hurting the people inside the house, some Palestinians started shooting from a distance. The settlers ran away and there was a heavy exchange of gunfire with the soldiers."[19]

I asked Hourieh if she wanted me to walk over and bring her over to my house. "No, that's fine. I just needed to talk to you about it. My family's whole house is in a shambles Muna. I'm so scared the settlers will return at night. How am I going to fall asleep?"

Before midnight, there were reports on TV about an Israeli bombardment, with LAW missiles, of the Palestinian Force 17 (Arafat's Presidential Guard) offices outside Salfit, near Nablus, where Hourieh's sister-in-law lives. There were reports also of a heavy

[19] October 11: For three days, large groups of settlers rampaged through Palestinian villages and towns in the West Bank and inside the Green Line, burning down Palestinian homes, vandalizing parked Palestinian cars, throwing stones, shooting at Palestinian drivers, and attacking Palestinians. In Jenin, Nablus, Bethlehem, Hebron, Khan Younis and Rafah, Israeli settlers attacked school children on their way home from school today. In some instances, Israeli settlers shot at children near their schools. The Israeli Military Authorities declared Nablus a closed military zone. Israeli settlers attacked several villages around Nablus, including the villages of Yitmah and Howarrah (source: Addameer human rights group: http://www.addameer.org/september2000/).

exchange of gunfire in the area. Three more Palestinians were killed by the end of the night, one of them in Tulkarem. There were reports of another person tortured to death by Israeli settlers. I haven't followed the details yet but will know in the morning. So this brings the number of Palestinians killed today to five. Have we reached a total figure of 100 victims, or is it 98? I am losing track.

Meanwhile, we all continue to feel a strong sense of despair and anger at the international community. Governments around the world are silently watching us get butchered, while much diplomatic effort is being spent on reaching a deal with Hizbullah regarding the three captured Israeli soldiers. The lives of Israelis always count; they sure get leaderships around the globe dancing on their toes.

Israel's closure of the West Bank and Gaza Strip continues. We are prisoners in the Bethlehem area. Some things, like my brand of cigarettes, aren't getting delivered. Because of the rampages of the settlers, it is unsafe to take back-roads to travel around the West Bank and therefore many people can't get to work. We are cooped up, each in the tiny bantustan zone we live in. And Israel may just let the closure extend for a considerable period of time, in order to collectively punish us all for resisting an ugly and heavily armed military occupation.

In the meantime, on some Gulf satellite stations, there are live broadcasts of campaigns to collect donations for the Intifada. We sit and watch the fundraising on TV. Will this mean that the nearly 3,000 Palestinians who've been wounded or maimed will be well taken care of and provided with all the care and rehabilitation they need?

Ask this question around Dheisheh and everyone laughs, laughs, and laughs. Why not stop pumping oil to the West for one month as a donation to the Intifada? Why delay holding the Arab summit until the 20th of the month?[20] Why wasn't it held already as a

---

[20] Arab leaders gathered in Cairo on October 20 for the first Arab summit meeting in six years. Libyan President Muamar Qaddafi walked out of the summit in a pre-planned move over the Arab states' failure to take a clear and united stance on freezing relations and ending normalization with Israel. During an October 18 live interview on the Qatari-based al-Jazeera satellite TV, Qaddafi embarrassed Arab leaders when he unexpectedly read parts of the final declaration to be adopted at the summit, which did nothing more than "denounce and condemn" Israel for its aggressions against the Palestinian people. Qaddafi asked whether the angry Arab man in the street is going "to content himself with these types of empty communiqués which limit themselves to denouncing and condemning Israel" (source: news reports).

donation to the Intifada? Why not invest money to buy shares in large Western media corporations as a donation to the Intifada?

But then again, why has Israel managed to capture Palestine in 1948, occupy the rest of our country in 1967, and get away with it all these years if it is a tiny state surrounded by "hostile Arab nations?" Why?

*   *   *

Thursday, October 12, 2000

Dear Diary,

When the first Israeli bomb was fired on Ramallah, we watched it live on the Qatari-based, al-Jazeera satellite station. Then we watched as more bombs descended on Ramallah, Gaza, and, later – exactly one hour after Israel announced the end of its "operation" – more bombs on Nablus, Hebron and Jericho. All the while, nothing stirred or moved out on the streets. All of Palestine was watching Barak go totally insane.

My husband, Ahmed, and I had friends over to watch TV with us. I kept going next door to the neighbors' and coming back. The phone kept ringing. Friends were calling from Jerusalem, Ramallah, France and the States. What could we say? If Barak wants to declare war against an unarmed Palestinian population, what can we say? If Israel, a nuclear power to be reckoned with, is telling us that its operation today is just a "token", then what can we say?

As the raids on Gaza and Ramallah came to an end, thousands of people in Ramallah, Bethlehem, Dheisheh, Nablus, Gaza, and I don't know where else, immediately took to the streets, marching and chanting, "Barak we are not afraid." What is there to fear? More bombings? More massacres? More beatings? More arrests? More destruction? More statelessness? What can the Israelis dish out at us that they haven't been already dishing out at us for the past 52 years?

More than two decades of Israeli occupation had left the West Bank and the Gaza Strip in a state of infrastructural ruin. Inadequate electrical generators which couldn't deal with the growing consumption; a too small to mention number of phone lines for households and businesses; a lack of properly paved roads; a lack of sidewalks that could keep us from competing with moving cars for space on the streets; an insufficient number of schools, hospitals, colleges, and more, so much more.

Then, starting in 1994 and 1995, when Israel started redeploying from parts of the West Bank and Gaza Strip, we started seeing, slowly, but surely, a building process all around. True, we're still at the beginning stages of putting this place back together, and the streets of the Palestinian Territories, wherever you go, are still littered with garbage, building debris and litter, but we were beginning to slowly and surely get somewhere in terms of making this a nicer place to live.

When angry Palestinians killed two members of the Israeli undercover units in Ramallah this morning, we paid close attention to the news. There was tension in the air and most of us thought that Israeli snipers might heat up the situation by killing more demonstrators, or some such thing. But to start bombing buildings in the middle of residential neighborhoods wasn't something we imagined Barak would be crazy enough to do. Police stations in Ramallah, al-Bireh, Gaza, the governor's office in Ramallah, official offices, Palestine Radio and TV transmission towers, the still-under-construction Gaza port, an electric generator in Ramallah, cars, and more, were all bombed during Israel's latest show of military might.

And so now, not only do we have to deal with the massacre of 105 Palestinians and the injury and maiming of 3,000 Palestinians during the past 13 days, but also with the destruction of all the hard work that has been put into rebuilding Palestine. It is all too much to take.

As a result of Israel's bombardment, there were no phone lines or electricity in parts of Ramallah. Israel has interrupted the transmission of the Palestinian mobile phone system, and for several hours, I couldn't even use my Israeli-operated mobile phone. The Israelis have jammed the transmission of all cellular phones used in the Palestinian Territories. The radio announcer tells us that according to the Ministry of Supplies in Bethlehem, there are enough food supplies in the Bethlehem area to last one month but the supply may expire sooner because people are buying and stocking up on food just in case the situation worsens.

I haven't stocked up on food and have enough in the house to last for only a few days. Somehow, I neither have the energy nor desire to care about food. If the situation escalates, and I do worry that it will worsen following tomorrow's noon prayer, then who knows how Israel will respond! Should we get another taste of Israeli bombs, there will be no place to go. Unlike the Israelis, who are well prepared for war, we have no shelters and thus no place to hide. And with Israeli tanks positioned at every hole and every entrance to Bethlehem, from all directions, there is no way out.

But if the situation worsens and the unthinkable happens, all of us in the camp will deal with it together, as we always do. Those who are meant to survive will survive and those who are meant to die will die. There isn't much else that an unarmed population, with no emergency plan, no evacuation plan, or any other plan, can do. Believers put their faith in God. Being secular, I put my faith in the world stepping in on time to save us from total destruction.

So many people around me think we are heading toward regional warfare. They want the Arab countries to intervene and bomb Israel and to hell with it, as they say. I disagree. In the heat of the moment, people don't realize what a regional war really means. Should we reach a stage where Damascus, Amman, Tel Aviv and Cairo all start getting bombed, it will be ordinary people who will pay the price. Leaders never die in wars; they escape to safety. But mothers, fathers, grandparents, and children, they are the ones who pay the price as we have seen in so many wars in the world before. There are peaceful ways to bring Israel's massacres and its occupation to an end. A clear and united Arab statement announcing the severance of ties with Israel; the closure of all Israeli representative offices in Arab countries; and stopping or reducing oil exports to the West until Israel stops its atrocities and agrees to the establishment of an independent Palestinian state in accordance with U.N. Resolutions 242, 338 and 194.

Without clear Arab support, since we're not getting it from the United Nations, the United States, nor the European Union, the Palestinian population here will face total eradication should the situation worsen and should Israel step up its bombardment. What will we fight them with if they direct their tanks at our neighborhoods? With stones, or with machine guns? Can either bring down Apache helicopters or destroy Merkava tanks? I called Gaza tonight and spoke to my friend Samira in Shati Refugee Camp. Shati is located right across the Gaza port that was bombarded earlier in the afternoon.

"Where did you hide when the choppers flew overhead?" I asked.

"I didn't hide. I went out on the roof with my brothers Ahed (aged 5) and Ala' (aged 7) to watch," 15-year-old Samira replied. "Oh Auntie. It was awful. We watched as their bombs destroyed the port.

I felt so, so sad. They were still constructing it and it was beginning to look so nice and we used to go there for picnic lunches. Why did they have to destroy it?"

Samira, like my neighbor Muyasar, couldn't stop talking about the politics of the situation. Samira, who only a few months ago, had dropped out of school at the age of 15 in order to get engaged, couldn't stop criticizing Kofi Anan, Madeleine Albright, Bill Clinton, and Ehud Barak! Could this be the start of our women's great awakening?

Are women beginning to realize that making men happy by cooking for them and washing for them and catering to their every need isn't what the whole world is all about? Are women beginning to realize that without them, the men can't fight for liberation alone; that women have to play a role, and have to be armed with the knowledge, the education and the skills in order to play a role?

Listening to Muyasar and Samira speak gives me hope and makes me believe that there is a shining light at the end of this very long, eerie, and dark tunnel.

* * *

Tuesday, October 17, 2000

Dear Diary,

I haven't been able to write for the past four days. The headaches, the nausea, and the pain in my eyes finally caught up with me and I started to feel a terrible lingering depression whenever I sat at the computer to work. I couldn't write, just as I couldn't keep any food down, or escape the persistent nightmares whenever I tried to sleep. Friends getting injured, blood, and people seeking shelter from falling bombs. Even when we sleep, there is no escape.

But there is no escape from writing either. Writing is my morphine; it is the only outlet left for me these days. Too much happens around us each day, yet somehow, we must go on and keep at it. We have to find survival mechanisms, and go on. Those of us who don't die from bullet wounds and falling bombs, develop high blood pressure, heart conditions and ulcers. I call Dr. Ghada at the Beit Sahour Medical Center and she tells me I ought to go visit her clinic and see the sort of ailments patients are seeking treatment for.

They're all ailments caused by stress, tension and frustration. And in the past few days, we've had a lot to feel frustrated about.

Following Israel's bombing of Palestinian towns last Thursday, October 12, and Arafat's subsequent decision to attend the summit with Barak in Sharm el-Sheikh, a general depressed mood descended on all of us and has lingered since. It is a depression mingled with anger. Anger at a summit that expects Arafat to "end the violence" – as if it is Palestinian Apache choppers, tanks, high-velocity machine guns, snipers and armed settlers which are aimed at Israeli civilians rather than the other way around. Is the world's logic so hopelessly warped out of shape! What's wrong with you, world?

If Ariel Sharon hadn't "toured" the grounds of the al-Aqsa Mosque on September 28, the al-Aqsa Intifada wouldn't have started, and nearly 120 Palestinians wouldn't have been killed and nearly 3,000 more wouldn't have been injured. If Israeli soldiers hadn't killed two Palestinians refugees at the Lebanese border on October 7, Hizbullah wouldn't have abducted three Israeli soldiers, and the crisis wouldn't have taken on a new and more dangerous twist.

If Israel hadn't sent an undercover unit to Ramallah on October 12 to assassinate God-knows-who in the Palestinian Authority or Fatah Movement, then an angry mob wouldn't have killed them and our towns and cities wouldn't have subsequently been bombarded. If Israel hadn't forcibly occupied our land back in 1948, then things would be so much different now. Yet while Israel initiates the violence, kills, maims, bombards, imposes blockades, Clinton asks Arafat to stop the violence! Is he a sane person doing the talking, and we are the insane ones who are doing the listening? Or is it the other way around?

For days now, nobody has been able to stop talking about their anger at Arafat for agreeing to go to Sharm el-Sheikh, to demand the withdrawal of Israeli troops and the lifting of the blockade! Arafat shouldn't agree to meet with Barak until Israel shows a willingness to end its occupation of the West Bank and negotiate an honorable, permanent peace agreement.

Is this what we are asking for? To bring back the situation to what it was like prior to the eruption of the al-Aqsa Intifada? Are we really, after the spilling of so much precious human blood, expected to go back to settlement expansion, house demolitions, Israeli-issued permits that control our movement, economic control, arrests and detentions? Is this what we want to go back to? Are we being presented with either the choice of ending the resistance and accepting, unconditionally, Israel's apartheid state so we can live happily ever after as Israel's obedient "niggers"? Is our other choice to get the hell bombed out of us and then get accused of "starting the violence"? Oh world! This is the twenty-first century. Where is the logic?

Wake up world! Wake up Israel! When an unarmed population is cornered with guns, tanks, military planes and gunboats, the threat of death becomes so real that one stops giving it a second thought. And how can we give it a second thought? We have no army, no air force, no marines and no nuclear weapons to fight back. Our homes have no shelters, no first-aid kits, and we have no national evacuation plan. What are our real choices? To sit and die, or to die defending ourselves against this insanely aggressive massacre that no one seems willing to stop.

How about asking the world to admit that the sort of peace agreement that Israel and the U.S. were trying to forcefully shove down our throats is not a peace that can last because it would only create an apartheid Israeli-controlled Palestinian state and not an independent Palestinian state? How about asking the world to admit that any peace agreement that falls short of implementing U.N. Resolutions 242, 338 and 194 will never bring real peace to Palestine?

As I sit here writing, nearly 20,000 people are participating in yet another funeral procession in Bethlehem. The martyr this time is 14-year-old Muayad Jawarish from Aida Refugee Camp, Bethlehem. An Israeli soldier shot him in the head while he was on his way home from school, his school bag still on his back. Before the marchers lay Muayad's body to its final rest, all TV stations move to live coverage from Sharm el-Sheikh and the final summit statement.

A grim-looking Clinton tells us, indirectly of course, that a decision has been made to stop our Intifada. Instead of telling us that Israel will stop its continued massacre of the Palestinian people, he tells us that, "both sides will act immediately to calm the situation." He declares that Barak and Arafat "accept that there will be an immediate ceasefire and a pullback of Israeli forces to their positions prior to the latest wave of violence." Aren't ceasefires reached between two fighting armies? Well, answer me!

What calming of the situation, President Clinton? By the end of the day, three Palestinians have been killed, one of them shot by Israeli settlers while picking olives in his field near Nablus, and scores more have been injured.[21] Meanwhile, Israeli troops fired LAW missiles at Palestinian homes in Rafah Refugee Camp in the southern

Gaza Strip. A heavy exchange of gunfire near Beit Jala led to the death of an Israeli soldier and the Israeli military demands, through loudspeakers, that Palestinians in the area vacate their homes because Israeli tanks and helicopters were preparing to shell them. Luckily, there was no shelling, at least for now. After m4ourners laid Muayad Jawarish to rest, they chanted, "Arafat come back, come back, we are a people who won't kneel." Then they cursed Arab leaders and the Sharm el-Sheikh Summit.

All day today, Israeli military helicopters and unmanned reconnaissance planes drove us crazy, flying overhead non-stop, non-stop, non-stop. A show of military might to intimidate the occupied. I swallow more pills but don't feel better. Then I succumb to the tears again.

When Muayad Jawarish was shot yesterday, Israeli soldiers were using such high-velocity machine guns against demonstrators, and with such intensity, that the .50-centimeter high-velocity bullets penetrated the windows of the Beit Jala Government Hospital several blocks away. One young man was injured in the chest, as he was sitting in his parked car in front of a grocery store several miles away from the clashes.

No exposed areas are safe anymore, and yet there are no signs that world leaders are on the brink of pressuring Israel into stopping its savage military aggression against an unarmed civilian population. Meanwhile, Barak announces that lifting the blockade depends on

---

[21] October 17: As the final statement of the Sharm el-Sheikh summit was being drafted, Farid Massassrah, 28, from Beit Farouk, Nablus was shot dead by Israeli settlers while picking olives in his family's olive grove. Israeli settlers, under the protection of the Israeli military, attacked Palestinian farmers harvesting olives in their orchards in Beit Farouk, firing live ammunition at the farmers. Farid was shot in the head with live ammunition, and three others were injured, including Farid's cousin, Majdi Issa, 42, who was shot by live ammunition in his chest, and remains in a critical condition.

October 16: In Silwad, on the outskirts of Ramallah, Israeli settlers under the protection of the Israeli military set fire to a five-dunum olive orchard. The owners of the land were unable to put out the fires in time to salvage the olive trees. Israeli settlers are reported to be attacking Palestinian cars with stones on roads outside of Ramallah.

October 16: Israeli settlers, protected by the Israeli military, this evening attempted to attack the village of Harres, near Nablus, with at least two Palestinians injured, including a 7-year-old. Palestinian security sources reported today that all entrances to villages in the Salfit area have been sealed with cement blocks (source: Addameer human rights group: http://www.addameer.org/september2000/).

stopping the Intifada in the next 48 hours. How, after all this, are the Palestinians expected to have faith in international efforts to bring genuine peace to Palestine, now or ever?

Another day passes and no one believes or wants the Intifada to stop. The struggle for liberation has been going on for five decades. During all these years, young girls have grown up and become mothers; and mothers have become grandmothers. They've buried too many husbands, fathers and sons, and still we are not liberated; we are still under occupation and we still don't have an independent state. How many more generations of grieving mothers have to suffer before the world realizes that occupation cannot last for ever? This time around, the Palestinians have had enough of Israeli aggression, of American acquiescence, of a biased Western media that has not dared use the word 'massacre' in its coverage, and of an inept Arab leadership, which couldn't care less even if we bled to the last drop.

Welcome to another day in Palestine! Rise and shine to another day of occupation and try to find yourself a place under the sun. It is there if you look for it. And so are the green pastures, the blue sea, and the rainbow on the horizon. Just stretch your neck out further and you'll find it.

*   *   *

Wednesday, October 18, 2000

Dear Diary,

I'm beginning to enjoy the evenings at our house. Friends, neighbors and relatives drop by to drink coffee, watch the news, analyze the latest developments, watch more news, and share the impact that the Intifada and the blockade have had on our lives. Having people around helps ease the pressure, or share it, at least.

Firas, Marianna's uncle, looks thinner and more restless than usual. The father of two very young blind children, he worries about not having any income at the end of this month. He works with Adeeb and Naim, both from Dheisheh, in construction in Bethlehem but with the blockade, there have been no shipments of cement, and therefore no work.

Since there are no social security and unemployment benefits available to anyone in Palestine, Firas, his wife, and children will have to eat their meals with his brother's family until the situation improves; as if it is only by food alone that man survives. Wajieh, Ahmed's cousin, is luckier. He has an office job and will have a salary at the end of the month. But after three weeks of not being able to go to work in Ramallah, he is beside himself with boredom.

"I can't concentrate enough to read or to potter around the house. All I can do is just sit there and watch the news all day. I feel like such a wreck," he complains. Boredom is eating people alive.

The phone keeps ringing. Friends call from Nablus, Ramallah, and France to check on us and make sure we're safe. We call friends in Rafah, Gaza, and Nablus to make sure they're safe.

We hear on the news that starting tomorrow morning, Israel will lift the "internal" blockade imposed on the West Bank. We all start to laugh. All that this "internal" lifting of the blockade means is that people who live in Bethlehem's Zone C will be able to travel to Zone A. All the villages surrounding the town of Bethlehem are in Zone C and therefore under full Israeli control. As a result of the blockade, residents of these areas have not been able to leave their villages, only minutes away from downtown Bethlehem, and drive to town. Now they can. Big frigging deal! The main blockade, preventing any of us entering Israel, or traveling from the southern to the northern part of the West Bank is still in effect. This means that people still can't go to work. It means that doctors, nurses, teachers, university students, employees, construction workers, patients, and many more, who need to get to Jerusalem or to their jobs inside Israel, remain unable to do so.

And even if we can now take back-roads to move around the West Bank, we know how the Israelis operate. We've lived through blockades before. There'll be so many checkpoints on the roads. Cars will be held up for extended periods of time while identification papers are checked, and arrests will be made. We'll have the Israeli military there again to remind us that we still live under occupation, and that Israel is in control of the land.

Good morning, occupation! And a very good morning to you too Sharm el-Sheikh! Are we supposed to be happy that the resistance of our people is being squashed so we can go back to life under occupation? Just like that!

I ask Wajieh if he plans to take the back-roads to get to his office in Ramallah tomorrow and he says no. There are settlements on the way and he can't be sure what the situation will be like. I tell him I don't plan to go to my office in Ramallah either until I am absolutely sure that it is safe.

We switch the channel to Israel TV. A woman, full of gay smiles, is telling her audience about the newest movies being shown at Israeli movie theatres. "This is a must-see film," she says sweetly. Wajieh and I look at one another and laugh. We live in such a crazy, crazy world. Life goes on in Israel. It is as if it is a nation on the other end of the earth that has nothing to do with what happens in the Palestinian Territories. It is as if the Israeli soldiers who've been bombarding, shooting, killing and maiming Palestinians these past three weeks are some mercenaries from planet Venus and not part of the nation that occupies us with such brutal force.

Hourieh calls in the afternoon to complain of headaches, nightmares and pains in her stomach. I ask her to bring along her three kids so we can go for a walk. Maybe some exercise will help clear our exhausted hearts and minds. We walk for nearly an hour and a half and the whole while, a small, remote-controlled reconnaissance plane flies around overhead, reminding us that there is no respite. Along the way, we don't see too many trees, and certainly no flowers; just litter, building debris and garbage strewn everywhere. I don't know why we can't clean up Palestine. If we love our land so much and are dying for it every day, why can't we at least keep our environment clean?

We take Marianna with us. She runs around, giggling and having the time of her life. At the end of the walk, we go to Hourieh's house for tea. Marianne climbs up my chair, throws her small head on my chest and immediately falls asleep. I stroke her hair and struggle not to cry, deeply touched by just how much she feels safe with me. Oh, Marianna!

Hourieh tells me that the settlers' attack on her family's house the week before has resulted in damages worth 30,000 shekels (about U.S. $7,500). There is no insurance of course and no funds allocated by the Palestinian Authority to compensate people for any damages done to their homes, their cars, or businesses.

But then material loss seems so insignificant. A Palestinian doctor interviewed on the radio says that of the more than 3,000 Palestinians injured in al-Aqsa Intifada, 400 are permanently handicapped and will need years of rehabilitation. Yet there are only two rehabilitation centers in the West Bank, only two! So how will all these people get proper, long-term rehabilitation?

When I turn on the computer to check the email in the evening, I do a quick chat with Iyad over in Khan Younis Refugee Camp in the southern Gaza Strip.

"How are things over there?" I type.

"Forty-eight injured today, eight in critical condition, four clinically dead, and two paralyzed after being shot in their spinal cord," writes Iyad. After a brief silence, he writes, "This is what they want at Sharm el-Sheikh."

When will the main blockade be lifted and when will people be able to move between Gaza, Jerusalem and Israel, no one knows. Even when it is lifted, no Palestinian can enter Israel without applying for Israeli-issued entry permits. We all suspect that the list of Intifada activists, who will be considered a "security risk" and denied entry permits, will be in the tens of thousands.

Another Intifada, more mothers with dead sons, more wives without husbands, more kids without fathers, and the Israelis expect us to meekly return to where we were before the start of the Intifada: to being a herd of quiet sheep, grateful to live under occupation. The only alternative they offer us is the slaughterhouse, and nothing else.

*   *   *

Thursday, October 19, 2000

Dear Diary,

The emails keep coming. From women I know, and from women I've never heard of before. From male friends, and from men I've never met before. Emails from as far away as Japan, Iran and Pakistan and even an email from someone I don't know in Turkey. It seems, my dearest diary, that so many people out there read you and they leave me no choice but to fill your pages each day. I laugh and cry at the same time. I write these pages to keep my wits about me, and people out there read them to keep their wits about them too. Their daily emails of encouragement and support push me forward, and my words help them understand.

And here I am, the writer who's been wanting to write a book for years and even managed to get a contract from a London publisher, but always found one excuse after another as to why I couldn't do it. Here I am writing each day when my excuse for not writing has always been lack of time, fear of failure, fear of not meeting the challenge. Oh, how I sit here and laugh at myself now. I sit around in the same pair of pajamas for two or three days before remembering that I've forgotten to change my clothes. I don't even comb my hair anymore and all I want to do is sit here to send and receive emails and to write my diary, to say it all, to bring it all out.

Funny what happens to you when you live in this sort of situation, when you don't know when all hell will break loose and whether or not this is going to be your last day, your last meal, your last words, your last laugh. Funny how time becomes precious and how getting things done when you want to do them becomes imperative. I never know if I will live another day to write another entry.

Will there be a tomorrow for us? Maybe yes and maybe no. Who knows! As I write, I hear a heavy exchange of gunfire nearby. I don't even leave my chair. There are clashes a few meters away in the town of al-Khader. Oh, what a familiar sound it has become these past three weeks: trrrr tak tak tak, trrrr tak tak tak, and now I hear the helicopters too. So, things haven't calmed down even though Barak has given us an ultimatum of 48 hours to bring the Intifada to an end! Forty-eight hours or you'll do what, Monsieur Prime Minister? You'll send more tanks; your army will shell us some more; your snipers will kill more people? Death, and more death!

One of the TV stations advertises the airtime tonight for "Cry Freedom". Remember this powerful movie starring Denzel Washington and Kevin Klein? Sure you do. Remember when the movie was released, apartheid still existed in South Africa? Remember how we all cried when we watched it? Well! Apartheid in South Africa is no more; it is done and finished with. Black South Africans didn't die for nothing. Those who remained alive are now free.

Do you hear this Mohammed al-Dura? Do you hear me? They may yet make a movie about you, and how you died in the struggle to end apartheid in Palestine. So what if some Israelis are trying to blame you, the victim, by saying that your father didn't protect you well enough and this is why you died. So what if an Israeli official – was it Dani Yatom, the chief of staff – who said that you had it coming because you were part of the Intifada? They say you deserved to die Mohammed. Even our death they try to distort. They blame the victim instead of asking why soldiers shot a helpless boy and his helpless father to begin with. They do this so they can keep on justifying their apartheid rule of us.

Oh! Open up my heart, for there is still more pain to come. Open up my soul, for there is still more human tragedy to absorb. Open up, damn you. They're not finished with us yet. Their war machine isn't done with our human flesh yet.

Tomorrow if I am up to getting dressed and leaving the house, I may go visit Grandpa Attalla's grave over at the Lutheran Cemetery in Bethlehem. What a serene place they buried you in Grandpa, right under a huge pine tree. The smell of the pines is so soothing too. Oh, Grandpa! Remember your house on the Mount of Olives in Jerusalem; the one you moved to after the 1948 War? I remember it. Remember your beautiful piano and all the music you used to play for us? I sure do. You're lucky you're not here to see what the occupation has led to. Your land in Beit Jala is all confiscated, and an Israeli family lives in your old house, in what they now call West Jerusalem. It is all gone Grandpa and you left us here to fight for it alone. You took your tenderness with you, your gentleness, and even your music.

But South Africa is free now Grandpa. Did you know that? And one day when I come to visit your grave, your spirit will be able to tell if I and everyone else in Palestine have also been set free. I just know that you'll be able to tell. Your spirit will feel our freedom in the air. The sky will be bluer, the trees greener, and more birds will be flying around than usual. Oh, and yes, the sun will even be brighter and it'll shine down on us so hard that it'll penetrate our skin and suntan those spots in our hearts, where the chains of occupation have left their cruel marks. You'll also hear the music, and I'll learn how to play the piano just for you, just for you!

There was an explosion just now at the headquarters of the Palestinian Force 17 presidential guard offices in Bethlehem. Three people are dead and scores more are wounded. Reports say that a gas canister exploded and some ammunition was caught in the fire, which led to a bigger explosion. Other reports say the Israelis shelled the place. The cause is still unclear, considering all the commotion at the location right now. Reports say that there have also been Israeli threats since this morning to bomb the offices of Radio Bethlehem 2000 if the station doesn't stop airing "anti-Israeli propaganda". Imagine! Threatening to bomb a radio station because it broadcasts anti-war propaganda!

Welcome to Israel, the only democracy in the Middle East. Welcome!

If I were a devout Muslim, I would pray five times a day and read the Holy Quran. If I were a Christian, I would kneel at church, say a few prayers, light a candle and read the Bible. But being secular, I continue to have faith in the human race and its ability to take a strong stand and demand that Israel's occupation and apartheid rule be brought to a final end. We all have to believe in something.

The helicopters are back; they're flying closer, lower and circling round and round. They're bombing the village of al-Khader nearby. It's going to be a long night. I feel like throwing up. Friends called and are coming over. The dishes are waiting to be washed. The laundry out on the lines is waiting to be brought in, folded and put away. I should remember to eat too! I keep forgetting to eat.

Marianna and her sisters are out in the alley playing. Their giggles soothe me; they're so carefree. But the sound of the helicopter overhead suddenly deafens all other sounds. Some kids scream. I hear ambulances going by on the main road.

Bleed to the last drop, Palestine, and let the world watch and cry. Bleed rivers and seas and oceans, Palestine. You've been bleeding for 52 years and still no one sees your rivers, seas and oceans and how they've turned into one endless flood.

*   *   *

Saturday, October 21, 2000

Dear Diary,

I feel a change in me today. I look at everyone around me and each person holds a special beauty in my eyes. I pay close attention to people in a way I've never done before. Their eyes, their hair, their clothes, the way they cross their legs when they sit, their shoes, the color of their socks; details I never cared for before, but details that now seem so significant and, oh, so very valuable.

My neighbors Um Ra'ed, Ibrahim, and Firas come over. I ask them to drop by so I can show them the latest graphic photos of martyrs I received via email. They're dumbfounded by the sight of the ripped-open heads and arms, the torn flesh, the visible bones, the bright, bright red blood. Ibrahim moves away and sits at the end of the room. I, on the other hand, have looked at these pictures several times today. I feel obsessed with the extent of Israel's brutality, and keep looking at the photos, again and again. I neither want nor wish to forget the brutality, or let it slip my mind, not even for a fleeting moment. Perhaps opening that particularly graphic email at 4:30 this morning was a mistake. Maybe it screwed up my mind! But, hey, wait a minute here, my mind doesn't feel screwed up. In fact, it was after watching the graphic photos that everyone suddenly appeared so beautiful before my eyes. They're killing beautiful people for God's sake. And, any day now, it could be someone I love. It could be someone I know, ran into, or even shared a ride with. It could be a human being who didn't deserve to die, didn't deserve to have his life cut so short, so soon after finding a bride, or becoming a father, or graduating from school, or getting that one great promotion, or furnishing that new house. No one in the room speaks as I flip through the photos. They watch in silence, disgust and pain.

Afterwards, we sit to watch the news and drink instant American coffee. I pay close attention to Firas's facial expressions and his hand gestures as he speaks and I think, ever so quietly, and without anyone hearing me think, that I should memorize how he looks. Then I glance over at Ibrahim and think the same and then I turn my eyes to Um Ra'ed. God! The cloth of her embroidered dress seems especially bright today. Did she just wash it? What sort of detergent did she use? Or has it always been so bright and I just didn't notice before? I wonder!

I wonder if these people that I care about will still be here in the next days and weeks. I wonder if I will be here too. I don't understand why I'm not afraid. I feel such a variation of emotions in the span of a single day, but not fear. Why God? Why aren't I afraid? Is it because for three weeks now we have been so saturated with the sight of death that it doesn't frighten us anymore? I don't think that's the reason. So what is it then?

Oh! It is the people around you, stupid Muna! It is the children, the women and the men. It is all these beautiful people around. It is all these beautiful human beings who need to eat, sleep, use the toilet, earn a living, bathe, and go shopping each day. It is all these human beings who need to do everything that distinguishes them from the dead, you stupid, silly, goofy woman! It is all these beautiful, unprotected people around you that you cannot help, that you cannot protect, that you can only love, and laugh with, and share pain with, and enjoy being alive with. For tomorrow may or may not be another day.

Marianna runs over to me, jumps in my arms, and starts squeezing my cheeks with her small fingers.

"Who is your love?" she asks me as she rubs my nose with hers.

"Your grandma Um Ra'ed," I tease.

She closes her eyes, throws her head back, broadens her face with a big smile, then throws her arms around my neck, kisses me on the lips and says: "No, no, no, I am your love."

I hold her tight and feel a surge of strength move from her body to mine. I feel the strength of an undemanding and unselfish love. Oh Marianna! Oh my sweet, darling, little Marianna!

Yesterday I couldn't write. I didn't have time to write. It was Friday and I made myself turn off the computer at 10:00 a.m. I needed to spend my day differently than I had spent it these past three weeks. Watering the plants and feeding the birds was my second plan of action. My first was turning off the radio and TV. No listening to the news for me today. What could happen anyway?

But the phone keeps ringing. Friends who want to talk, and foreign journalists who need help with one thing or another. I make an appointment to go with an American journalist to Beit Jala in the afternoon, to interview someone from the Fatah Movement. Until that time, I occupy myself by doing nothing, nothing at all. And all the while, I feel so proud that I managed to not listen to the news. Oh, so proud!

By 4:30 p.m., I'm done with the American journalist. I say goodbye at the Beit Jala–Bethlehem intersection and decide to walk the several blocks to Maher and Marina's house. Maher is my husband's cousin and Marina his Russian wife. Both are very close friends of mine. The sky is black and rain appears to be on the way. Maybe if it comes, it'll wash away Israel's aggression with it.

As I walk, I realize just how deserted the streets are. Deserted in a very gloomy kind of way. Bethlehem has been in mourning following the death of two Palestinians in the explosion at the Force 17 headquarters in Bethlehem on October 19. No shops are open, there are no people around, and a lone car every now and then drives past me. The area feels eerily empty; and then the light drizzle starts touching my face. I never realized what a soothing effect drizzle could actually have on my eyelashes, my lips, my cheeks, and my neck. I never noticed these tiny little drops of life.

As I walk through the door, Marina asks me if I've heard the news. I tell her, ever so proudly that I haven't listened to the news all day.

"But six Palestinians have already been killed today," she gasps.

For the next three hours, a heavy headache bangs at my head. I sit on the couch quietly, watching the news, chain smoking, drinking coffee, and listening to, but not participating in, the conversation around the room. Hind, Maher's cousin, can't stop talking about the first- and second-graders she teaches at school.

"The children are too terrified to walk home from school and don't want to carry their school bags on their backs," she says. "They think the soldiers will shoot them like they shot 12-year-old Muayad Jawarish the other day. One of the kids in my class saw him as he lay there on the pavement with his brain spilled out on the street."

My headache gets worse and worse and worse. Hind's father, Tawfiq, lifts his 18-month-old granddaughter. Dalia is blond and very pretty. She wiggles in her grandpa's arms. He picks up a pretzel from the plate on the table and brings it close to her mouth. She giggles, grabs the pretzel and bites on it. He hugs her and puts her down – and they say Palestinians don't love their kids and that's why they send them off to throw stones and die! So how come all I see around me in the room is love, an ever so ordinary family sharing love? How come? Tell me you damn Israeli soldiers with your missiles, tanks and guns!

Events start developing rapidly in many parts of the West Bank and Gaza. There are clashes everywhere[22] and Apache helicopters are shelling Beit Sahour. We watch the bullets whizzing by in the sky and we watch the explosions live on Manger TV. Then we hear a real explosion. An Israeli tank just fired a shell on Beit Jala, and the sound of the explosion reached Maher and Marina's house in Bethlehem.

At 7:30 p.m., shortly after the bombing started, my husband Ahmed, Maher, Marina and I get in the car and drive to Beit Sahour to watch the bombing. Along the way, on the dark streets of Bethlehem, we see tens and tens of Palestinian policemen and security forces. Young men, so very young, are unable to sleep at their military headquarters for fear that they will get bombed. They seek shelter in vacant buildings, and doorways. Poor guys! The Palestinian Authority, with all its money, doesn't send anyone around to give them hot drinks and hot food.

As we approach Beit Sahour, we see many cars parked along the sides of the roads and people standing there watching the clashes down the hill. I don't know why scenic points in the States suddenly

---

[22] By the end of the day, four Palestinians were shot dead, including one who was shot in the head by an Israeli settler (source: Addameer human rights group).

come to my mind. I am talking about these scenic spots you drive to, and sit in your car to watch a breathtaking view of the city before you. That's what came to my mind. Except the scene here is different. We are watching a town, engulfed in darkness as Israeli Apache helicopters fire away at residential neighborhoods. Nothing moves. There is no panic, no screams, and no people running away. Mommies, daddies, babies, boys, girls and grannies all sit in their homes, in total darkness, and endure the shelling.

There is no other place to go. If you're lucky you're not hit, and if you're unlucky, you're hit. There is no third alternative.

As we drive from Beit Sahour to Beit Jala and then back to Bethlehem, Marina moves closer to me in the back seat, puts her arm in mine, rests her head against mine and says in her broken Arabic, "Oh Muna! We are here today, but tomorrow maybe we won't be here. Tomorrow, maybe we die."

"So lets go home and eat," I say. "This way if we die, we will die on a full stomach," I joke, trying to ease her tension.

Marina caresses my belly, smiles, and asks me, "Are you hungry?"

"Famished," I reply, "so let's not die on an empty stomach."

"Maher and I should move to Moscow and you should take Ahmed and go to America," she tries to sound optimistic.

"But what will the people who can't go anywhere do Marina?" I ask her.

She shivers and moves closer. "Oh Muna! Are we going to die?" she asks.

"I don't know Marina. We might. Are you afraid?" I ask.

She shakes her head and looks out the window. I look out the other window. We both sigh and stop talking.

Later at night when I get home, I drop in to check on Um Ra'ed.

"I don't think I have my wits about me anymore," she says, exasperated.

"Why is that?" I ask.

"I used dishwashing liquid to fry eggs for my son Khaled tonight. I couldn't figure out why the oil was so foamy and wouldn't heat up. Can you believe it?" She laughs. "I am so absent-minded that I reached for the dishwashing liquid instead of the cooking oil."

"Don't worry about it," I smile. "I go to the toilet and then five minutes later, I forget that I went already, and I go back into the bathroom and don't remember what I'm there to do."

I tell myself that we are normal! Besides, dishwashing liquid makes the eggs taste better and if they're sunny side up, then oh yummy, the Palmolive brand makes them even sunnier, with a more shiny yellow. The type of yellow that warms even the coldest of hearts, but not the dead ones, not the ones that are already in the darkness under the ground. Oh no! Not those. For down there, there are no colors, no sunny-side-up eggs and no souls on the verge of losing their minds.

*   *   *

Tuesday, October 24, 2000

Dear Diary,

Go away! Stop! Leave us alone! Cease your bombing. Enough! How many more seconds, minutes, hours, days, nights, and weeks do we have to endure your guns, helicopters, tanks, tear gas, and bullets? How many more people do you have to kill under the pretext of "defending" your security? What about defending our security? Who will protect us from your slaughter? Who? No one it seems will raise a finger to bring Israel's onslaught to an end. Absolutely no one: not the international community; certainly, not the United States; and most definitely not the Arab leaders.

Do you detect despair in my voice? Well do you? What do you expect? I'm tired of feeling like throwing up, of the headaches, of crying when my friends and neighbors talk about their pain, of being so darn tired all the time. I am tired of feeling so helpless! It was those damn helicopters, hovering endlessly overhead the night before last that got me to be in the state I've been in these past two days. They were bombing Beit Jala, Beit Sahour and Aida Refugee Camp. They were flying so low and then there came the sounds of the explosions. Was it 9 p.m. when I awoke to the sound of the shelling? Was I fast asleep to begin with? I don't remember anything anymore.

As I lay in bed trying not to think about the terrible pain I felt in my knees, I realized just how frightened I was. My heartbeat was racing as if I was running in a marathon. The helicopter felt like it was in the room with me. I felt like I was in a game of Russian roulette. What is their next target? Will Dheisheh be on their list tonight? Will our house get bombed? Should I get out of bed and try to hide somewhere? Where?

I couldn't think of a safe spot in the house. Perhaps standing next to those two bookshelves in the study would be a good place. No windows near and perhaps the bombs won't find me there. Or should I hide under the bed?

Silly thought. Only children hide under beds, and as a child in the 1967 Arab–Israeli War, I hid under the bed in my family home in Amman. I'm too old for that now and we've been through too many wars already. Enough! Enough world! Why don't you step in and put an end to this atrocity? Just end the occupation! That's all that has to be done. End the damn occupation that won't leave us alone. The occupation that chases us around more closely than our own shadows; relentlessly crowding in on our little space, and killing us!

Ten Palestinians were killed by Israeli army gunfire this last Friday, then five were killed on Saturday, then four on Sunday, I don't remember how many on Monday, and the number is three, so far, today. It is only around 10 p.m. The night, as they say, is still young. If you live under occupation in Palestine, it means that the night is so young that anything can happen. Today can be the very last day of our lives. This is the persisting thought on everyone's mind. We think about death, about dying, about not being alive, about getting killed, about ceasing to exist, and we think about it all the time.

Yesterday afternoon, I went with some Swedish journalists to Beit Jala to look at the homes that Israeli tanks had shelled the night before. As we stood out on the street and it started to rain, Mia, a Swedish photojournalist and friend, urged me to seek shelter from the rain. I grinned idiotically and told her: "But it is nice to feel the rain on my face. This could be the last time that I stand in the rain." She stared at me blankly and didn't say anything.

Everything we do each day feels like it is being done for the last time. It is a game of Russian roulette I tell you! Do you know how to play, or would you like me to show you how? Answer me! Do you want me to show you how to play? It is easy really. Oh yeah! So very easy! Ask the three- and two-year-old Nazzal brothers in Beit Jala and they'll tell you how to play. They'll tell you how they were in their bedroom playing with their toys one minute and the next minute the room was wrecked by an Israeli shell. The bomb came right into the bedroom and exploded. Just like that! But the Nazzal brothers have a smart mommy who's pretty good at the game of Russian roulette. She intuitively took them out of the room a spilt second before the shell came tumbling in.

The foreign press descended on Beit Jala like kids descending on, oh, what is it called? Why can't I remember things anymore? I'm talking about that place in California! What's it called? Oh, it comes to me now, Disney Land. The press came to Beit Jala en masse just like kids going to Disney Land. They stuck their cameras, microphones, and notebooks in everyone's face and asked, "The Israelis say that they've been shelling Beit Jala because armed Palestinians fire shots at the settlement of Gilo from residential neighborhoods in Beit Jala. What is your reaction?"

Excuse us! Say that again! Ask us again! What was your question?

How many Israeli civilians have been killed since the start of the al-Aqsa Intifada? How many Israeli civilians have been wounded? How many Israeli homes have been shelled? How many? Answer me you objective people! You journalists, who are so interested in covering "both sides" of the story. For that's what we are to you, another news story. Here today, gone tomorrow! We are the nameless, faceless, ageless Arabs who are easy game; like gazelles during hunting season. Oh boy! Is it that time of year again? But the world doesn't shake to our death. No earthquakes! No threats to boycott Israel! Who would dare?

Oh, dear me! Here I am being silly all over again. Who cares if the Israelis bomb the hell out of us Palestinian niggers? We deserve it, don't we? This, after all, is what happens to those seeking freedom and independence. Someone has to step in and grind our noses to the ground and show us who is master.

The problem is that we refuse to die. Even in our death, we are still alive. Mohammed, Rufaida, Mustafa, Ali, and thousands of others who've died for the sake of Palestine in these past 52 years, all live on! They live in the hearts and minds of their children, their grandchildren and their great-grandchildren. They live in the air, in the soil, on the trees, in the sky, in the clouds, and always in our hearts and minds.

Type, my fingers, type! Think, my brain, think! Hurt, my heart, hurt! Throw up, my stomach, throw up! Throb, my head, throb! And do get used to it. This is only the beginning of more days and more weeks to come. The Israeli war machine is definitely not done with us yet.

I cheat just now. I can't stand listening for the sound of the helicopters and I am sick and tired of running to the window whenever I hear a sound. So I put the headphones on and play some pop music, real loud. Oh hello, pop music! It has been a very long time. I've missed you. You resemble a normalcy I no longer know. You resemble what real life should be like but is no more.

A few songs are all I get to listen to before Ahmed taps me on the shoulder. I remove one earphone from my ear and listen to what he has to say. They're bombing al-Bireh next to Ramallah right now. And here I thought Ahmed was tapping my shoulder to ask me if I wanted to go out to dinner, or go for a walk and sniff the roses, or catch a late-night movie, or, even, go listen to some jazz!

Oops! Excuse the slip. For a moment, I forgot that I am in Palestine. We don't do these kinds of stupid, normal things here. Rather, we wait to see if we are going to die. That's the sort of serious stuff we're into. Bombing, shelling, more names of the dead, someone who's 22 now, then someone who is 12; a human being from Gaza now, and then a human being from Tulkarem.

Count Muna, always count. Count so you don't forget how to add the numbers. Soon you may not know what one plus one adds up to. Count and throw up! Throw up and count. Lose weight, if you like. Lose your mind too, if you dare. This is just the beginning. They have not killed enough of us already. The blood of the dead and the wounded doesn't even fill someone's swimming pool yet. Not yet!

Tomorrow is another day. Will we wake up or won't we? Will we live or won't we? Will we lose an eye, an arm, or a kidney? Will we be amongst the survivors? Will we live to talk about it? And if we do, will anyone listen. Will they?

Hello! Are you out there? This is Palestine calling. P-A-L-E-S-T-I-N-E, you people out there!

*   *   *

Thursday, November 2, 2000

Dear Diary,

I felt drawn to her the moment I saw her. She was sitting on a ledge at the end of the long staircase leading to her rooftop apartment. Her eyes were downcast and her hands rested listlessly in her lap. As I reached the end of the staircase, she slowly lifted her sad eyes and looked straight at me. Our eyes locked, and I felt a knot in my throat as I greeted her. She barely murmured an audible hello and went back to staring blankly into space. As I stepped onto the third-floor terrace, I was aghast at the sight that greeted me. Charred clothes, burnt remains of family photos, freshly picked green olives, blackened shoes, handbags and pieces of furniture were strewn all over the once white floor tiles.

"Oh my God!" I muttered under my breath as I approached what once was someone's house but now stood burnt and gutted. On top of one pile of burnt clothes, the family had placed a round, green plastic bin. Inside of which were two LAW missiles, a semi-round tank rocket and smaller pieces of shrapnel and other smaller missiles.

"This is what they used to shell our house," said the elderly house-owner who runs a private hospital nearby.

"Who lives here?" I asked him.

"My brother and his wife. She's the one sitting over there on the ledge."

I turned my eyes toward her. Her eyes held mine again and she got up and walked over to us.

"This is all we are left with," she screamed as she pulled at her sweater. "The clothes on our backs are the only things left. I walked around the house like a mad woman, trying to salvage something. But even my gold necklaces, bracelets, and earrings had melted, so did our passports, our birth certificates, my identification card, and our furniture. Everything, everything except ..."

She abruptly stopped talking and walked away. I thought she was still in shock and couldn't handle talking anymore. But a few minutes later, she was back.

"These are the only two things that survived," she said in a pained voice as she waved two volumes of the Holy Quran in my face.

I was too shocked to speak and when she saw the tears forming in my eyes, she softened her tone and said, "This is the power of almighty God! The Quran is the only thing that survived."

The larger volume was a bit charred at the top left edge, but in perfect shape otherwise. The smaller version didn't even look like it had survived a fire. It was in excellent condition.

"This volume [the larger one] was in the living room, and this one [the smaller one] was in the bedroom. They are the only things that survived their bombing," she moaned. I was too overwhelmed to speak. The young woman abruptly walked off again. I walked over to the railing, wanting a moment to myself. On the rooftops of the houses around, I could see the shredded pieces of red bricks. The impact of the bombing on the house was so severe that pieces from the red-brick roof had flown down to the street and also reached several nearby rooftops. Many windows in several houses were broken. On the rooftops around, I could see satellite dishes that were gutted, as well as solar water heaters, and water reservoirs. On a nearby hill, only a few yards away, I could clearly see an Israeli army tent; a tank lurked nearby. This is the location from where a Merkava tank leashed its rage at Palestinian homes. The distance was way too close for comfort.

"Instead of withdrawing their tanks as agreed upon between Peres and Arafat, they dug ditches early this morning, hid the tanks, and pointed their guns away from our homes," remarked the owner of the house.

I turned around and started looking more closely at the mess on the floor around me. Parts of a girl's face smiled at me through the charred remains of what once was a happy family photo. A plastic toy duck sat in a bucket of blackened water. Was a child playing here before the bombing? I wondered.

Welcome to the village of al-Khader, a short walking distance to the south of Dheisheh. Yesterday, Israel lashed out in what is considered its most vicious air and tank attack in the Bethlehem area since the start of the al-Aqsa Intifada more than one month ago. For three hours, Israel went on a savage bombardment of al-Khader in order to evacuate six Israeli soldiers who had gotten trapped and wounded in an ambush during armed clashes in the village. Two of the soldiers were killed; unable to go in and evacuate them, the military went into a rage, firing air and ground missiles at the village for three hours, non-stop. Then after the soldiers were evacuated, the bombing continued for another three hours and included, in addition to al-Khader, Beit Jala, Beit Sahour and Aida Refugee Camp.[23] It was the first time that the Israelis didn't forewarn the Palestinians that they were going to bomb.

[23] November 1: Israeli settlers and soldiers attacked the village of al-Khader in the morning. Four schools were forced to close when the settlers prevented children from reaching their schools. Mohammad Al-Hroub, 27, an officer in Force 17, was killed in al-Khader, and twelve Palestinians injured following an exchange of gunfire between Palestinian police and Israeli soldiers. An Israeli officer and a soldier were killed in the confrontation, and four Israeli soldiers were lightly wounded. The Israeli military then used tanks and heavy artillery fire against the village. Later in the afternoon, at least two Israeli attack helicopters randomly shelled residential areas in the village, killing Wa'el Ghneim, 26, who was standing in front of his home. At least ten other homes were damaged, and two homes were completely burnt. The attacks continued for several hours. Ambulances came under direct heavy machine-gun fire, preventing them from reaching al-Khader. At least seven Palestinians were reported to be in critical condition. Late in the evening, Marwan Assaf, 21, from Wadi Fukin, Bethlehem, was reported killed. Early in the evening, heavy artillery, tanks and attack helicopters were used by the Israeli military to shell the towns of Beit Jala, Beit Sahour and Aida Refugee Camp. Several homes were damaged and many residents were injured. Attacks continued late into the evening (source: Addameer human rights group: http://www.addameer.org/september2000/).

The air and ground bombing was so heavy and came from so many different directions that some homes at the edge of Dheisheh were hit. Using the mosque's loudspeakers, we were asked to keep off the streets, off rooftops and away from windows. I was next door with little Marianna and her family. We had no way of telling how the situation would develop and whether or not the shelling would include Dheisheh.

I remember feeling restless and wanting to go home to try and protect something at the house. Should I hide the computer, or the TV, or my personal papers? If I hide my computer in the bedroom, maybe the bedroom would be shelled. So, should I leave the computer in the study? Swift thoughts kept flying through my head, but I had no answers. Soon, I realized how fruitless it was to try and do anything. I couldn't decide what to try and save. Were personal belongings like photo albums and private papers more important? Were the most expensive electric gadgets more important? Or was everything very important?

As I stood on the terrace of the burned house, I thought about all this; about my desire to protect what I owned. I realized then how the young woman who survived with nothing but the clothes on her back must feel. People work so hard to purchase what they have. None of it comes easy. When we buy a new refrigerator, neighbors come over for tea to share the moment with us. When we put new tiles in an old bathroom, it is a major event and friends come over to admire the bathroom's new look. And then, just like that, to see everything burnt to the ground is the hardest feeling ever.

Earlier in the day, I go to Aida Refugee Camp and visit some of the homes that were shelled there. The grandfather is a former schoolteacher and must be in his mid- or late seventies.

"They think that if they bomb us, we will flee our homes. But, never again! We did it once in 1948 and again in 1967. This time, we are staying put. And if they think that we are going to go somewhere, then the only place we are going to go is back to the village we left behind in 1948. Otherwise, we are here to stay; we will not become refugees a third time," he says heatedly.

I look at the old man and wish I could run over to him and hug him. That's the spirit and the resilience that the Israelis can't understand, and don't wish to understand. The women and children gather around and everyone starts chattering at once. Someone makes tea, and the grandmother tells how she hid in the kitchen with all the other women and children in the family.

"The children hid their faces in my lap and kept screaming as the helicopters fired away overhead. But I kept telling them to put their faith in God. God will protect us."

Some young boys show off the empty missile and high-velocity bullet shells they gathered after the bombing. I don't know why looking for Easter eggs as a child came to mind. The enthusiasm was the same.

Later in the afternoon, and while still in the village of al-Khader, we hear ambulances go by. "The Israelis just killed a guy," someone says. We race to the Beit Jala Government Hospital. A crowd is already gathering in the hospital's courtyard. We learn that the martyr this time is Yazan Halayka, aged 17. People look on as Yazan's brother and one of his best friends sit on the sidewalk in the corner and sob. Some minutes later, a car bringing Yazan's mother and grandmother pulls over. The wails of the grieving women force everyone to fall silent. They are the loud and painful wails of two women who cannot bear their loss. The women insist on going in and taking a look at Yazan. "He's already in the fridge. You'd better go home. May God give you strength."

The women resist, but a family member forces them to walk back to the car. The sight of the grandmother is too much to bear. Her hands hang stiffly in front of her bosom, as if they are paralyzed. She drags her feet, lets out a wail, and starts to violently shake her head. I turn my head away. The courtyard is full of young Palestinian men. How long do they have to bear this sight of heartbroken mothers? How long? How long? How long? Another day passes, with another martyr, another bombing, another air strike, and another funeral procession.

All around Dheisheh, life goes on. Someone fixes a leaky roof. Someone else finishes plastering his walls. A peddler walks around selling cheap honey-sweet pastry. Nasser, who was injured early on in the Intifada drives by in his car, waving at passersby who greet him and thank God for his speedy recovery. Two boys walk by arm-in-arm. Women hang the laundry out to dry and hose down the alleyways.

And everywhere in the West Bank, women and children climb up olive trees to shake the leaves and force the olives to fly down to the ground. It is olive picking season in Palestine. Bombing or no bombing, it is olive picking season in Palestine. Soon, we will dip our bread in fresh olive oil. Life goes on. The determination to live is unwavering. The determination to live a better life is unwavering.

Hourieh's daughters, Khloud, 11, and Sanabel, 9, ring my doorbell.

"We want to invite you to a barbecue tomorrow afternoon," they say through their giggles.

"And what would you like for desert?" I ask.

"Anything you like," they tell me. "You come get me tomorrow and we'll go get some pastry together," I say. They run home happy. I close the door happier.

It is the spirit of a people that Israeli guns can't kill. So you shoot away as much as you like. It is the spirit that you can never kill. On the contrary, in this Intifada, the Israelis have created another new and very young generation of Palestinians who don't want their occupation.

"What are you going to do?" I ask the owner of the burnt house in al-Khader.

Taken aback by the apparent stupidity of my question, he smiles, "Rebuild, of course. What else?"

I grin and walk away.

*   *   *

Monday, November 6, 2000

Dear Diary,

A couple of years ago or so, I interviewed an affluent Bethlehem businessman I know well for an article I was writing about the economic conditions in the Palestinian Territories. During the interview, Srour complained, among other things, about declining sales and the rising cost of living.

"What do you have to complain about? You are rich; you and your wife go on occasional vacations overseas. You never worry about your next meal," I offered.

Today, as I sit here writing my diary entry for the day, I find myself remembering Srour's answer.

"Imagine that you have a briefcase full of a million dollars," he said as he listlessly puffed on his cigarette. "And picture yourself a prisoner inside a cell, with the briefcase right there beside you. Would your million dollars do you any good?"

"I see your point," I replied.

"Money means nothing without freedom," he continued. "What is the point of having money, if you are a prisoner? And that's what we are, prisoners in our own land."

F-r-e-e-d-o-m! Where are you hiding? Come out and walk over to me. Come and open the door to my cage. Open it. Can't you? Is it locked? Well, pry it open damn you! Pry it open and let me fly away. Let me fly. Let me try my wings. And if they're too stiff after being incarcerated for so long, it is all right. I shall attempt to fly anyway. And should I fall, I shall get up, lick my wounds, and try again, and again, and again, until I finally make it up to the open blue sky. And once there, I shall soar up high, and circle, and soar again. Oh Freedom! Do open my cage door.

Why are you turning your back on me f-r-e-e-d-o-m? What is it? Don't you like the color of my feathers? Are they too dark? Or is it my identity that you can't stand? But I thought we were all God's creation! I thought we were all equal under the sun!

Does it matter if my feathers are black or white? Does it matter whether I'm a lovebird or an eagle? I still eat, sleep, and breathe! I breathe you damn fake! I exist. I have blood in my veins. I bleed if I'm wounded. I exist you moron. Oh F-r-e-e-d-o-m! Is it the prisoners that you don't like, or is it the jailers that you are so afraid of? Do they scare you away? Do their war guns frighten you?

Well don't be afraid. Come to me and I will show you that life without you kills fear and makes it so meaningless. Life without you is like a falling dead leaf in the autumn. Come to me and let's make it spring again. The buds are sprouting. Do you see them over there, far away in the distance? OK, so look harder. Do you see them now like I do? They're there on the other side. Make my bud sprout freedom. I smell so good when I'm in full bloom. Oh, so good! Don't you want the smell to fill your nostrils?

Why are you running away? Did someone tell you I'm Palestinian? Did they tell you about the Israeli blockade? Did they tell you we are prisoners in our small towns, villages and refugee camps? Are you afraid you'll be imprisoned too?

Oh, F-r-e-e-d-o-m. Don't worry about it so. It is collective you see. Collective punishment is what we call it. Don't let the term scare you. It just means that we are all riding in the same boat. So what if it is filled over capacity and is about to capsize? We'll make it to shore together. Come be our anchor. Please come.

Oh, where is your sense of humor F-r-e-e-d-o-m? So forget about the boat. Instead, think of us as a bunch of school children who've been very mischievous, and are now being collectively punished. We all have to sit here, and sit here, and sit here until her royal highness decides to let us out. Come sit with me at my desk. And no, the way to wait it out isn't to stare at the minutes of the clock ticking by. Do what I do. Let go of your imagination. Imagine what you would do if you were free; if you were outside. Just picture it: the schoolyard is covered with grass. Someone mowed it this morning. Can you smell that? Yeah! me too. The sun is warm, like a nice toasty fire on a cold night. A group of kids are playing soccer. Two are over there having a high old time on the swings. Do you see the light breeze blowing their hair? The core of an apple is on a window ledge. A pigeon is picking at it. A boy shouts. Startled, the pigeon flies away. The apple core drops to the ground.

And there on the ...

Hey, F-r-e-e-d-o-m, where did you go? Don't you like my story? But it helps pass the time. It helps keep the faith. It eases the pain of our collective punishment.

Are you off to work? Or is university that you attend? Or are you off to visit your uncle? Sorry I can't join you. None of us can. We are not allowed to go anywhere. We are being punished for desiring freedom. Thinking about things like democracy, independence and liberty always gets us in trouble, at least those of us who survive. Others don't make it you see. They are killed for having such thoughts. The rest of us remain sitting ducks. Quack ... Quack ... Quack. Bang! Another one bites the dust.

But life goes on damn it. Those who don't bite the dust manage to eventually swim away to safety. Believe me F-r-e-e-d-o-m, they really do. They make it through the snags and the rapids and they reach some safe waters somewhere. It doesn't matter where, so long as they are free. It may take seconds, minutes, hours, days, weeks, months or years, but everyone eventually makes it to you F-r-e-e-d-o-m.

Are you off for good? Are you too wimpy to open my cage door? Be that way. I don't need you anyway. I have nothing else to do and nowhere to go. I have time on my hands so, I shall eat away at the lock, and eat away, and eat away, until I get it to open and let myself out.

Look up you people out there! Look up from wherever you're sitting, laying, standing or walking. Do you see me? Hello, down there! I'm up here, high up in the sky. I'm that brown eagle, soaring and circling high above your head. My wings are spread wide. Oops! There goes one of my feathers; I see it slowly dropping toward you. I see it falling right into the palm of your hand. Nice catch! Now hold my feather close to your heart and someday, when you see a bird in a cage, look at my feather and think of me. And, yes, that's right, reach over and open that cage door. Don't hesitate. You can do it. We all can.

*   *   *

Friday, November 17, 2000

Dear Diary,

When I was a kid, around 6 or 7 years old, I used to go to Beit Jala with my grandfather. We mostly went on Sundays. We would take the bus from my grandparents' house on the Mount of Olives in East Jerusalem and go spend the day in Grandpa Attalla's hometown.

Grandpa Attalla was born and raised in Beit Jala, but he lived in Jerusalem most of his life. We would go to Beit Jala to visit his relatives, and of course, his land. A kindly elderly woman, I don't remember who she was, would pick some really delicious apricots from Grandpa's land, fill them in a big straw basket and we would take them back to Jerusalem with us. Eating apricots grown on our land always held such a special meaning. And of course, Grandma Marie always made us the best and tastiest apricot jam.

The smell of the freshly picked apricots, from such a distant past, lingers in my nostrils. It lingers because something about that smell makes me feel so safe, so secure and so protected from harm. Holding Grandpa's hand, I would walk with him and visit the family. Sometimes we would go to the Sunday mass first and we would almost always light candles in church.

A very caring and loving man, Grandpa Attalla always exuded a calming sense of serenity. I don't ever remember seeing him angry or unkind. He loved me, loved his land in Beit Jala, loved his hometown and without intentionally teaching me, he actually taught me to love it too. He taught me through his actions, and not his words.

And even though I lived outside of Palestine most of my life, Beit Jala remained etched in my mind as this quaint, clean and pretty town where the church bells always seemed to toll. In my heart, it remained a place where nothing bad could ever happen. It is also a place where part of me belonged; the part that longed for Grandpa Attalla and the long-lost past.

But my heart felt so heavy with sadness yesterday when I went to Beit Jala to attend the funeral of Dr. Harry Fisher, a long-time

German resident of the town.[24] I didn't know Dr. Fisher and had never, until his death, even heard of him before. But the hushed crowd outside the church, the somber toll of the church bells, the flags of various Palestinian political factions being waved quietly, the ominous feeling in the air were all just too much to take.

There is death every single day. There is death around us every single day. And each day brings different names, different ages and different places of residence, of people who went away for good leaving immense sadness and emptiness behind.

I had no heart to go to see Dr. Fisher's house. Everyone I ran into at the funeral kept urging me to go take a look. "The shell penetrated his body. Go see the pieces of his flesh on the wall."

I didn't want to go see the pieces of his flesh on the walls. Do I need to go see the pieces of his flesh on the wall in order to hurt, to feel sad, to feel angry, to feel helpless? No, I don't.

How much longer will the world stand – arms folded – and watch? When will the basic human right to life, the Palestinian's basic right to life, become an issue of concern? When will the excuses stop? When?

Here we have adjusted to the death, the shelling and Israel's ceaseless attempts to blame us for the "violence", the confrontations and the blockade. Suddenly, we the victims of occupation are made to appear as the villains.

The scenes of death are part of our daily lives. Who will remind the Israelis that they are occupiers? Who will make them realize that occupations don't last? Who will make them understand that Israel cannot exist without Palestine and that if Palestine is not free, then Israel can never live in peace?

As mourners bid Dr. Fisher their last farewells, I decide that I can't handle watching another family; another wife and more children mourn a loved one. So I walk up the hill to look at the houses that

---

[24] November 16: Attacks by the Israeli military with heavy machine-gun fire, tanks and helicopter missiles continued from 11 p.m. on November 16, until 5 a.m. on November 17, resulting in severe damage to numerous homes, including a nearby field hospital. Ambulances were prevented from reaching those injured because of the continuous shelling. One family was trapped in their home for several hours while their home was being shelled. Dr. Harry Fischer, a 50-year-old German doctor, married to a resident of Beit Jala and living in the village for almost 20 years, was killed while attempting to assist those injured during the attacks. He was hit directly by a tank shell, and died instantly (source: Addameer human rights group: http://www.addameer.org/september2000/).

had been shelled by Israeli tanks and helicopters a couple of nights before.

The narrow old roads, with the beautiful stone houses, appeared so deserted. Beit Jala, with its happy people; the kids riding bikes, the girls walking around, the women sipping coffee on balconies, was like a ghost town. No one was laughing. A second-storey house stared at me with its gutted windows. One of its walls split open by a falling shell. A car stood parked nearby with all its windows gutted and spread on the pavement. A girls' school stood empty and silent with no children around. Smashed windows and damaged walls added to my sense of gloom. Then more houses, with gutted walls and smashed windows and another car, all appeared before me as I continued to walk.

A young girl stood outside one house.

"What's your name?" She asked me in English, thinking I was a foreign journalist.

"I'm Muna, and you are?" I replied in Arabic.

"This is my house that they shelled," she said.

And that was it. She walked back to the broom that had been in her hand, picked it up and went back to sweeping the broken glass. Her parents looked on. Their faces appeared so desolate, uneasy, tired and full of despair. I couldn't find words to say anything to them, so I nodded a greeting, smiling faintly, and walked on.

Down the winding road, I could spot the settlement of Gilo across the hill, an ugly settlement built after 1967 on confiscated Palestinian land. It doesn't fit the beautiful landscape and looks more suited to suburban America. The Israeli military had erected cement blocks on the settlement's grounds. Some guys in Beit Jala tell me that these are the soldiers' positions, the locations they use to shell Beit Jala at night. Behind me, a newly built villa stood in shambles. The Israelis had bombed the hell out of it. Someone's new house is now no more.

All this because the Palestinians resist the occupation, want it to end and fire some shots that do very little damage to the settlement. A few Palestinian machine-gun shots that are met with air and land shelling bringing more death and destruction. Are we expected to feel threatened? Are we expected to succumb to force? Are we supposed to like the occupation and accept it as a *fait accompli*? What are human beings worth if they can't be free?

What is life worth if one loses the right to be free? Israel, the so-called only democracy in the Middle East, is the occupier of another people. So how come simple facts like that get lost, swallowed up, forgotten and discarded in today's world?

If the Palestinians had killed more than 200 – or is it more than 250 now – Israelis and wounded more than 3,000 in a span of less than two months, would the world have stood silent?

Oh! Don't fret so. Sadness comes and goes. But it is the determination, which lives on inside us at all times. It is the determination of an occupied people to seek justice, to seek liberty, to seek equality, and to seek a warm place for a people who yearn to have a cozy place under the sun. A place free of guns, free of soldiers, free of death, free of oppression, free of the ugly wrath of an uglier occupation that simply refuses to desist.

So hold on Beit Jala! Lick your wounds and move on. Bury another human and move on. Weep and move on. History is on your side. They will read about you someday in the history books, and someone will say that Dr. Fisher's mutilated body, and the pieces of his skin tissue on his living room wall and ceiling, were not plastered there in vain. Freedom doesn't come before pain.

So accept the pain you mothers, fathers, husbands, wives and children of Palestine. Accept the pain. There will be more of it to come. And then one day, you shall be free and white pigeons shall circle your skies. And ships shall sail to your Mediterranean port, and roses and jasmine shall blossom in your gardens.

And one day, if you come to Beit Jala, you shall see me there. You'll find me in Grandpa Attalla's land, planting apricot trees. And a kindly, elderly woman shall come to me with a straw basket and we shall fill it with the pungent fruit. And I shall take some in a clay bowl and I shall go sit by Grandpa Attalla's at the Lutheran Cemetery grave just up the street in Bethlehem.

And if you happen to pass me by, you shall hear me whispering something to his soul. If you walk closer, you shall hear me telling Grandpa Attalla that his love for his land has lived on in his granddaughter's heart. You shall hear me whispering softly to him that it is our love of the land that gave us the strength to continue the fight for liberation and become free.

And if you listen to the wind, you shall hear Grandpa's gentle voice telling me that he already knew that his love of the land lives on inside me. And you shall hear me asking him to tell me just how he knew. And you shall hear him laugh softly and tell me that he has always known because his soul has always been able to rest in eternal peace.

*   *   *

Monday, December 4, 2000

Dear Diary,

As the car started making its way down the dusty, narrow alley leading from my house to the main road, I couldn't look around. I didn't have to. There was no need for my eyes to capture the images in order for me to see what was there. My neighbor Um Maher standing by her front gate, chattering with acquaintances as they pass her by. Abu Mohammed and Abu Shaker sitting right outside Abu Shaker's damp, cheap apparel store, to catch some sun. Young school boys crowding Hassan's "Quick Meal" falafel shop, rushing to buy a sandwich that they can gulp down before the school bell goes off. Abdullah unloading the boxes of fresh produce from the roof rack of his car, and haggling with customers over the price of the zucchinis, or tomatoes, or red apples.

The car reached the main road, turned right and headed north toward the Bethlehem checkpoint. I closed my eyes and leaned my aching head on the back of my seat. I was a total wreck, but tried not to show it. I was leaving Dheisheh and no one in the camp knew I was leaving. I didn't have the courage to say goodbye. I just knew that if I had to embrace all the people I love and bid them farewell, then the pain of my departure would have been too great to bear and I would have probably opted to stay. And I could not stay. There were so many reasons why I had to go.

As the car approached the Bethlehem Israeli military checkpoint, the tension inside me felt like two strong hands choking the breath out of me. What if the soldiers checked my American passport and realized I didn't have a valid tourist visa stamped inside? What would I do if they decided to detain me?

My foreign friends in the car with me kept telling me that I could lie and say that my tourist entry visa into Israel is stamped on a piece of paper that I had forgotten at home. But I was so bad at lying to the soldiers that I knew I couldn't pull it off.

The checkpoint resembled a war-zone military compound on high alert. Tanks, jeeps, police cars and armed soldiers stood as a barrier between Bethlehem and Jerusalem. This is the military might that Israel uses to intimidate the Palestinians into believing that it has the power and is in control. I looked at the tanks with utter disgust.

Would the Israelis be so intimidating if they were stripped naked of their guns? Would they like the feeling of being equal, or is superiority so deeply engraved in them that they would feel lost without it?

A soldier ordered us to stop and my friend behind the driver's seat rolled down her window. I felt numb all over. But a quick glance at her foreign passport is all that the soldier needed to see before letting us through. Just like that! Foreigners with foreign passports have the right to go in and out of the West Bank, but not the Palestinians. The soldier didn't even bother asking me and the other foreign passenger for our passports. We were free to go.

Oh Israel! Wake up. Wake up and see what apartheid rulers you've become. Didn't anyone whisper in your ear that South Africa is now free? When are you going to listen?

A strong sense of relief, of guilt, of excitement and of anticipation engulfed me as the car drove deep into Jerusalem. I began to see a crack in my cage door and knew that after a few more hours, I would be on a plane that would take me to the United States, to a place where there is no blockade, no checkpoints, no occupation, no soldiers and no guns. But at the same time, being in Jerusalem made me feel such sorrow. Israeli men, women and children were so clearly going on with their lives as usual, leaving me with the sense that I was on a different planet. They had no checkpoints to hinder their movements, no soldiers shooting at them and no tanks threatening to blow them and their homes to pieces. I thought of Marianna, cooped up in Zone A of Bethlehem, when a whole world was out there, waiting for her beautiful eyes to see. Is she an animal? Is she a beast to be put on a leash? Doesn't she have the right to see the world too and to roam in it like the free spirit that she is?

Damn Israel's injustice. Just damn it to hell.

With several long hours to kill before my plane is due to depart for Washington, my friends take me to Tel Aviv and to West Jerusalem. And in both places, I am shocked by what I see. They've been lying to the world all along. All this official Israeli talk about wanting to guarantee the security of the Israeli public is one big lie, and so is all the talk of the Palestinian Intifada being a threat to the security of Israelis. Business was going on as usual in both cities. Restaurants were packed in Jerusalem and so were the sidewalk cafes in Tel Aviv. I had to remind myself that I was in Israel and not in the U.S., and there were those excruciatingly long moments when it was hard to make the distinction. It was just all too clear that the Intifada in the

West Bank had no impact whatsoever on the Israeli public. While Israeli snipers brought innocent lives to an end with the rise of each new day, Israelis were going to the movies, walking their dogs, jogging and doing whatever else people in a 'normal' society do.

The contrast filled me with anger. How could the Israelis enforce an inhuman blockade on an entire population, preventing people from going about their 'normal' everyday life? Do they honestly believe that caging the Palestinians will force them to kneel, to succumb and to surrender? Don't the Israelis realize that free men and women cannot be caged, and if they are, all they do is to think up ways to be free again!

The U.S. embassy in Tel Aviv warned me that the Israeli authorities at Ben Gurion Airport in Tel Aviv may either force me to pay a sizable fine for "overstaying my welcome in Israel" for a considerable number of years, or may altogether prevent me from leaving the country. I had been in the West Bank without a valid tourist visa since May 1995 and no matter how much I tried to get some form of residency approved by the Israelis, to live in my country of birth, they always had an excuse for delays.

In the end, I stopped caring whether they gave me residency or not. I mean, I was born in Jerusalem and considered living in Palestine my right. I didn't need Israel to legalize my residency there. I already existed there, with or without their consent. True, I couldn't travel to Gaza, Israel or abroad, but I existed nonetheless. Of course, I can't deny that the notion of paying a fine or being prevented from leaving the country terrified me. Friends loaned me money for the fine, just in case, but I didn't believe that the Israelis deserved to take the money. In principal, I was against having to pay a fine for staying in "my" country. It just defeated logic, any kind of logic.

So I was almost a total nervous wreck when I approached passport control at the airport. I didn't care what I had to go through, all I knew was that I had to be on that plane. My entire being and my existence depended on it. I suppose in the end, the gods stepped in and decided to have mercy on my soul. I had worked myself into such a state of anxiety that things at the airport went far better than I expected. There was no interrogation, no search of my bags. There was only the warning, the clear threat. Oh yes! The direct and blunt warning that I would face "very serious problems" if I ever attempted to return to "Israel".

The young passport officer who told me this must not have been more than 22. I looked at her and muttered, "OK," and that was the end of that. I had no interest in finding out what sort of problems I would face. The message was loud and clear. I was not welcome back. So what is new? What is new about us Palestinians being constantly reminded that basic rights are not ours to enjoy? What is new about Israel's arrogance in telling a people that their homeland is not their own? Nothing is new. Too many Palestinian generations have swallowed and vomited Israel's arrogance, and for longer than any of us care to remember. Life simply goes on, and so does our resistance, the steadfastness and the immense desire to be free, no matter what threats the Israelis dish out to us.

As I sit on the plane and look down on the white patches of clouds, I imagine that I am a little girl jumping from one cloud to the next. I feel as if the clouds are cushiony cotton, wrapping me in their softness. I close my tired eyes and doze off into a very restless and disturbed sleep. Fifteen minutes later, I hear myself sobbing out loud. Startled, I open my eyes and sit up in my seat.

And then the tears come and I find myself too weak to control them. I nibbled at my cage and got out. I walked away from a life that meant everything to me for ten sweet years. I left loved ones and close friends; a people that the world knows as the refugees of Dheisheh, but whom I know as individuals with hearts filled with different dreams and desires, but mostly a dream to be free. I know that without having them in my life this past decade, that today, I wouldn't be me. And none of them realize, not even my darling little Marianna, that they taught me many a valuable lesson about pride and dignity, about giving without taking, about resilience and about having the sort of spirit that refuses but to be free.

But all the loved ones and friends I left behind don't know that it was precisely because I had learned my lessons so well, that in the end, I had to leave. I had to walk away from a personal cage that I had put myself into and didn't know how to get out of.

And you know what my dearest, dearest diary! It was you who helped me to open my personal cage and fly away. For how could I write on your pages, reach so many people, and talk about liberation when I myself was not free? The contradiction just killed me inside. It ate away at my heart, piece by little piece, each passing day. And my silent pain felt like a sharp knife, twisting and twisting inside my bleeding heart. And I just knew that I could no longer write about freedom for my people if I myself were not free. For without self-liberation, what meaning does liberation hold? Tell me you silent, silent diary, what meaning does liberation hold?

I sit here in Austin, in the heart of Texas, where there is so much space around me. Adjusting to open space is an overwhelming adventure. I feel like a child. For space here lies before me without barbed wire, without tear-gas bombs, without blood and without pain. I look out the window at the squirrels and the crows and the birds, the green grass and the trees. And I constantly think of Marianna. She has never seen green grass and has never looked at the squirrels on the trees. I imagine her before my eyes, running carefree and trying to catch a bird with her small hands. And I know in my heart that her right to be, to live, to roam free is just so very, very basic. She has to have it. She just absolutely has to have it. There is no other way. My longing for her adorable little face pushes me forward. The pain of knowing that I will no longer be able to see her grow before my eyes will most definitely keep on pushing me forward.

But one day, when there is a rainbow in Palestine and lots of green grass, I shall go to Marianna and together we shall run in the open space around us and pick apricots from the trees. Together, we shall open the palms of our hands, watch a bird fly down and rest in their warmth and gently wrap it with our fingers. Then together, we shall set it free, watch it fly up to the sky, and enjoy the surge of liberation that overwhelms us as we do.

Do you hear me my darling Marianna? There will be a rainbow in Palestine one day and you shall be so very free.

PART TWO

2 Farewell Washington (1988)*

When the first Palestinian uprising, better known as the Intifada, against Israel's military occupation broke out in the West Bank and Gaza Strip on December 9, 1987, I was a pampered Palestinian living the good life in America. While Palestinians back home were changing the course of our history, I was working on my muscle tone at a local health club in suburban Maryland. While they were facing death and injury, I was dining out at my favorite Ethiopian restaurant in Washington's ethnic neighborhood of Adams Morgan. While their homes were being demolished, I was sipping beer with my friends at the Childe Herald on Dupont Circle. The Intifada was as distant from my life in Washington as Mars from Planet Earth.

But all this was on the surface. Underneath it all, I was restless and quite unhappy. It was emotionally painful for me to watch the news on TV and see Palestinian women, men and children lash out with nothing more than stones against heavily armed Israeli soldiers. The scenes simultaneously thrilled and upset me. I was thrilled to see that my people were rising against Israel's 20-year-long occupation, but I also was upset because I was stuck in Washington away from it all.

Without realizing it, I became hooked to my TV set. Like an obsessed maniac, I spent hours taping all network television news coverage of the fast spreading confrontations. Then, in the evenings, I would invite my small circle of Palestinian friends over for a replay and watch while my male friends sobbed like children. Later, alone, I would lie on the sofa and play back the tapes until I had every scene memorized by heart. My sense of pride was simply awesome! For it was Palestine's children of the occupation, not the leadership of the PLO, or its freedom fighters, who were standing up to heavily armed soldiers and shouting – with stones – enough is enough. I could not help but think what a mockery these Palestinian children were making of our political leaders, our guerrilla fighters and our intellectuals. Since June 1967, when Israel occupied East Jerusalem, the West Bank and Gaza Strip, the Palestinians, whether armed with a gun, a pen or an olive branch, have been grappling to gain world

---

* (First published in *The Link* by Americans for Middle East Understanding, May–June 1999.)

opinion. But there were very few people in the world at large who really seemed to give a damn about us. The world's indifference had become commonplace. What if we were an occupied, stateless and homeless people? Nobody cared. Rather, much of the world continued to believe that we were terrorists while Israel was a small democracy struggling to survive in a sea of hostile Arab states. The entire world community had put the Palestinians on a shelf and forgotten about us. At best, we were considered homeless refugees; at worst, we were treated like a bunch of wild-eyed fanatics bent on the destruction of the Jewish State. Reality and image had become transposed somehow. And then BANG! The Intifada came and took everyone by surprise. No one anticipated the rise of the children of stones. No one imagined that Palestine's children of occupation would grab world public opinion and twist it to our favor. All of a sudden, the image of Israel changed. Scenes of armed Israeli soldiers firing at Palestinian civilians brought us more in world sympathy and support than the efforts of the PLO and its allies combined.

My need to be there with the Palestinians at this very critical period in our history was so urgent that I could not concentrate on anything else. I became moody, irritable and reclusive. By the spring of 1988, my spirits had hit rock bottom and I could not shake the dark cloud of depression that seemed to linger over my head. I started hating my life in Washington. I hated McDonalds, hated TV shows like *Good Morning America*, hated the *Washington Post*, and hated going to cocktail parties at Arab embassies and uttering shallow words like "nice to meet you" or "have a nice day". Most of all, I hated my impotence. Palestinian kids, some as young as seven, were picking up stones and throwing them at Israeli soldiers armed with lethal ammunition and tear gas. Their courage made me feel totally helpless and inept. I did not have the courage to face guns head-on like these kids did. I was a coward, afraid of death. I could never stand a few feet away from a soldier, his loaded gun pointed directly at me and threaten him with words, let alone with a stone. But damn it! I wanted to. I desperately wanted to be as bold as the young boys on my television screen.

My reasons were selfish, of course. I craved courage for no other reason than to conquer a lifelong fear, my fear of death. Death, which came when I was a child and took away my favorite uncle, my grandfather, and then, later, my best high-school friend and my father. Death, which left me feeling so cowardly, invariably afraid of losing loved ones, and incapable of dealing with the emotions of my loss. I could see that the Palestinians back home were dealing with death every day. Daughters were losing fathers and wives were losing husbands. Their sorrow did not seem to be less felt than mine and their pain appeared to be just as grave. Yet their close encounter with death did not hold them back. Instead, they seemed to be lashing out at it and challenging it every time they took to the streets and confronted the armed soldiers. Ashamed of my cowardice, I craved their courage.

My bout of depression and self-pity lasted through the first six months of the Intifada. Throughout this time I felt like a bad swimmer in the middle of a turbulent sea, wanting badly to reach the safety of a shore but not knowing exactly how to get there. I don't recall hating myself as much as I did back then. Just when I knew I had reached the edge, destiny came to the rescue again. It happened one hot and humid Washington afternoon in 1988 and it was my Palestinian friend Karim who unwittingly snapped me out of my depression.

Karim was a brilliant Palestinian writer and every week or so, we would meet at the Childe Herald, a popular pub that played Sixties music and served sumptuous hamburgers and salads. Over food and drinks, Karim and I would exchange news and views on the latest developments of the Intifada. Karim did most of the talking, using extremely sophisticated and eloquent words. I listened to him as intently as a pupil listens to a great teacher. On that fateful afternoon, I sat on my wooden bar stool smiling and nodding my head as Karim analyzed the situation back home. Suddenly I was struck by an odd feeling, a sort of a *déjà vu* if you will. I had heard these words before, all of them. Karim was repeating himself, I thought to myself, so why was I listening to him?

I looked deeply into his face and saw something new: a man who drank too much and a writer too self-absorbed to be as productive as I knew he could be. It was like looking in a mirror. If I did not do something soon to get out of the rut I was in, I would become like Karim. And I knew I did not want to sit out my Palestinian existence in a Washington pub until it grew too late for me to make a difference.

I threw up when I got home. I had had enough. I wanted out of my depression and self-pity before it was too late. My mind was set. My only chance of survival, of reaching the shore, was to get myself over to the West Bank. Nothing else was going to make me feel better.

Another six months passed before I boarded the plane to Tel Aviv. I had to become an American citizen first. According to Israeli law, Palestinians who carry passports from Arab countries cannot enter Israel unless an immediate family member in the West Bank or Gaza Strip submits an official request with the Israeli authorities on their behalf. Then it is up to the Israelis to approve or reject the request. I had a Jordanian passport and lived in the United States as a permanent resident. I did not have immediate family members in the West Bank.

As an American, however, I could enter Israel any time I wanted. The irony of the situation did not escape me of course. Being an American would give me easy access to my country of birth whereas my identity as a Palestinian born in Jerusalem would deny me that right. The decision was easy. If becoming an American could get me home, then I would become an American. And I did. The process at the department of immigration lasted from June until December 1988. And on December 13, I stood before a United States district court judge and pledged allegiance to the American flag. That same morning, I went to the U.S. Passport Agency and applied for my very own American passport.

Three days later I was booked on a flight to Tel Aviv.

I was in heaven. The entire planet was not spacious enough to hold me. Exactly one year and seven days after the outbreak of the Intifada, I was finally on my way home. I was going to watch the stone-throwing with my own eyes, smell the tear gas with my own nostrils and hear the sound of gunfire with my own ears. I was going to be part of something terribly frightening and terribly real. My life was about to have meaning. I was about to be part of something far greater and far more important than myself.

3   Welcome to Dheisheh (1990)*

The confrontations outside our front gate grew alarmingly intense. A hail of fast-flying stones made a loud thumping sound as they hit the concrete pavement. "Come here you sons of b———!" yelled the *shabab* (young men) from up the road at the soldiers who stood sheltered from view behind our metal gate. "Come here, you cowards."

To this, the soldiers answered the Palestinian youths with a round of live, rubber-coated metal bullets. The sound of the bullets whizzing overhead was sobering. They were so darn close. More stones flew in the air. A windowpane broke. A branch from the lemon tree snapped and fell to the ground. Our courtyard, now sprayed with stones, resembled a battlefield. The four rooms of our small house led to one another through the open courtyard and the front gate was the only exit to the street. But the soliders were standing right behind it. We were trapped.

During a momentary lull, Ahmed, my husband of less than six months, and I darted out of the kitchen and ran to the bedroom. It was the farthest room from the gate and relatively the safest. On the way, Ahmed looked in on his elderly mother. Too heavy-set to rush out of one room and dash into the next, Um Subhi sat crouched in the corner by the bed with a peeled onion in her hand. The Palestinians had discovered long ago that sniffing a peeled onion lessens, even if mildly so, the effects of tear gas on the respiratory system. "Stay here," Ahmed commanded her. "I'll be back." Um Subhi nodded and murmured, "May Almighty *Allah* damn them to hell!"

The shooting persisted. A bullet hit a water reservoir on a nearby rooftop and we could hear the sound of gushing water.

Suddenly the air in our bedroom was becoming impossible to breathe. "The soldiers are tossing tear gas into the courtyard," warned Ahmed. "Quickly, get a blanket and place it under the door." Before I had a chance to reach for the blanket, Ahmed's hand was pulling at the doorknob. "I have to get my mother," he yelled. But the moment he opened the door, a thick white cloud of tear gas forced

* (First published in *The Link* by Americans for Middle East Understanding, May–June 1999.)

him back into the room. "Dear God! Mother is going to die," he panicked. "Hurry! Cover your face with a scarf and get me one too."

With only our eyes visible, we started out of the room. I couldn't breathe. There was too much poisonous gas in the air. My mother-in-law's bedroom, less than six feet away, felt like it was at the other end of the earth. By the time we reached her door, I was in a very bad state. My eyes burned like hell and I couldn't stop coughing. "I have to get some air! I can't breathe! I can't breathe," I shouted at Ahmed as I ran to the front gate and swung it open. I preferred to get shot than die of suffocation. But the soldiers were gone.

I don't remember how I reached the house next door, but when I opened my eyes, I was stretched out on the floor underneath the ceiling fan. Um Ra'ed and her children were crouched beside me and someone was splashing perfume on my face. I started to laugh and cry at the same time. I couldn't believe I was alive. My face and eyes were on fire and I started to cough. "Ahmed! Where is Ahmed?" I screamed, jumping to my feet. By the time he reached his mother and started walking her out of the house, the soldiers had come back and wouldn't let Ahmed and his mother leave the tear gas-infested house. "Go back in there and die," the soldiers shouted at Ahmed as they pushed him back inside the gate and banged it shut. Luckily, the living room was the room least affected by the tear gas and Ahmed and his mom took refuge there until the soldiers left again.

It was November 21, 1990. I remember the date well because it was my thirty-first birthday. I will never forget that I almost died on my birthday.

For nearly a week we coughed, sneezed and felt a burning sensation in our fingertips whenever we touched anything in the house. Our blankets, kitchen utensils, and clothes were laden with tear-gas residue. Such was life in Dheisheh during the Intifada.

In March 1999, a group of Palestinian and Israeli graduate students paid me a visit in the camp. They were in a joint Israeli–Palestinian "peace" studies program and wanted to tour the camp. As soon as I started recounting incidents from the Intifada, one of the Israeli students interrupted. "The Israeli soldiers had no interest whatsoever in what was going on inside the camp," he said. "All we cared about was protecting the main road parallel to the camp which thousands of settlers used every day to get back and forth to Jerusalem."

"You talk as if you were here," I remarked. Staring me right in the eye, the young Israeli admitted that he had indeed been a soldier in Dheisheh for quite a stretch of time. "And all the time when the soldiers stormed into people's homes, beat them up, wrecked their furniture and tossed the hot meals that they were about to eat on the floor, they did it to protect the settlers?" I asked, agitated.

"Look," he protested, "I was in Shati Refugee Camp [in Gaza] on the first day when the Intifada broke out. We could have easily shot 200 people on the spot and ended everything there and then. But we didn't ..."

"How generous of you not to kill 200 so you can wait and kill more than 1,000 instead," I interrupted angrily.

The Intifada wasn't just about throwing stones at the occupation army. It was a reaction to a savage attempt by the soldiers of one nation to humiliate the men, women, and children of another nation. And this humiliation, which occurred at every hour of the night and day, is something that the Israelis refuse to understand. No human being succumbs to humiliation. It is part of human nature to fight it back.

What do the Israelis know about what the Palestinians go through at the hands of the occupation anyway? One of the most difficult things for a Palestinian during the Intifada was to witness, let's say, a violent demonstration in East Jerusalem and then walk up the street to the Jewish sector of the city. While the Palestinians down the road were being beaten and their shops forcibly closed, by Israeli soldiers and police, their civilan Israeli counterparts were walking their dogs and drinking cappuccino at outdoor cafes. This contrast never failed to amaze me and always left me with the sense that our occupiers were not Israeli fathers, husbands and sons, but some mercenaries from a far-away land.

This Israeli indifference, in my opinion, has played a major role in widening the gap between the two peoples even after the signing of the peace accords. For example, after a suicide bombing occurs in Jerusalem and Tel Aviv, the Israelis get up the next day and go to their jobs and schools, whereas the daily life of the Palestinian population, in its entirety, is interrupted because Israel always punishes the Palestinians collectively for the suicide bombings. In contrast, an Israeli settler like Baruch Goldstein can walk into a packed mosque and kill and injure dozens of people without disrupting the life of a single Israeli.

It is precisely at these moments, when Israelis like the student-soldier express such blatant indifference and arrogance, that I wonder what Anne Frank would think if she were to see what sort of occupiers her people have become!

What, I wonder, would she have thought had she been with us in Dheisheh at two in the morning that bitter cold winter night? Ahmed and I were asleep in our warm bed. Suddenly a mad banging on the front gate awakened us. Knowing it was the soldiers, but not knowing what to expect, we let them in.

"Get out here!" the officer barked at Ahmed. And for the next three hours, Ahmed, Saeed, Mahmoud and all the males in the neighborhood were forced, at gunpoint, to whitewash the political slogans written earlier in the evening on all the concrete walls. The women, standing at their windows, watched in the dark, apprehensive that their husbands or sons might be beaten or taken away.

The ice-cold air flapped through the men's flimsy pajamas and their fingers could hardly hold the brushes and buckets of white paint. Anyone who refused to obey was certain to be hit with rifle butts until his screams awakened all the sleeping babies and hard-of-hearing grandmothers in the entire block.

Saeed resisted that night. We all watched as the soldiers shoved his face on the pavement and then squeezed it with the soles of their boots. The rifle ends did not spare a spot in his body. Steady, hard blows, one right after the next.

"You're going to kill him," pleaded Um Saeed as she rushed toward her son. "Go inside you whore!" spat a soldier as he grabbed her by the hair and dragged her away, pushing her hard against a nearby wall.

Then suddenly, the stones started falling from all directions. Dheisheh was awake and fighting back, always fighting back. "Come here you b-a-s-t-a-r-d-s," yelled the *shabab*. "Come here and fight like men you sissy sons of b————," they screamed into the night in half Arabic and half Hebrew. The soldiers raced after them as they called for reinforcements over the wireless. Moments later, Israeli jeeps started driving in. The Israeli soldiers had their reinforcements, and the camp was now wide awake.

Welcome to Dheisheh, Anne Frank!

4   Urging on the Scuds (1991)*

During the Gulf War in January 1991, the Israelis accused us of being heartless. They claimed that while Iraqi scud missiles were falling over Tel Aviv, Palestinians in the West Bank and Gaza Strip were standing on their rooftops, whistling and laughing, urging on the scuds. The Western media picked up on this, their coverage of the war implying that we enjoyed watching Saddam's missiles spread panic and destruction into the heart of Israel.

Having spent the war in Dheisheh Refugee Camp in Bethlehem – when the entire West Bank and Gaza Strip were still under complete Israeli occupation – I know the Palestinians were misunderstood. No one outside the occupied territories had the vaguest idea what we were going through.

On January 16, one day before the war started, the West Bank and Gaza Strip were placed under Israeli military curfew. In Dheisheh, the curfew didn't matter much because the camp had already been under curfew since January 2, following severe confrontations with Israeli soldiers. What mattered was that camp residents had no way of getting ready for the war, especially as this was going to be the first war possibly involving chemical and nerve gas weapons, and the first time ever that people had to wear gas masks.

We heard about the gas masks, of course. We saw them on Israeli TV every night, and watched how Israeli citizens were instructed on how to use them. But the Israeli military authorities never issued us any, and while some Palestinians living in West Bank cities received gas masks, none were distributed in any of the 28 refugee camps in the West Bank and Gaza Strip. Therefore, we knew that for the duration of the war, we would have no real protection from chemical or nerve gas. If Saddam Hussein had actually used either, it is very likely that more Palestinians than Israelis would have died.

Shortly before the war, a Palestinian health organization distributed leaflets in the occupied territories instructing us on how to make homemade gas masks. We were told to place barbecue coal inside a hot oven to clear it of carbon dioxide. After cooling, we were to smash the coal into tiny pieces and place it on a piece of gauze,

* (First published in *Palestine Report*, January 16, 1998.)

cover it with another piece of gauze, and stitch the two pieces together. "In the event that chemical gas is used, cover your nose and mouth with the coal-enforced gauze," the leaflet read.

It also instructed us to wear long pants, socks, long-sleeved shirts, and heavy jackets. To prevent the gas from seeping through from the ankle or wrist areas, we were to wear plastic bags on our feet and plastic gloves, securing the edges with seal tape.

Meanwhile, the Arabic service of Radio Israel instructed listeners on how to seal a room in the house, to make it chemical gas proof. We were told to buy rolls of plastic sheeting and seal tape, and secure the windows and doors of one room in the house. We were further instructed to stock up on canned food and bottled water. It all sounded so simple, but it wasn't.

The curfew we had been living under in Dheisheh since January 2 was lifted on the morning of January 14 and clamped down again on January 16. Everyone in the camp had precisely two days to buy everything they needed. Yet most residents faced a serious problem: there was no cash flow.

Dheisheh had been placed under curfew off and on since the previous October. This meant that people were out of work for a good part of three months and many were going through some deep financial hardships. My husband, Ahmed, and I were of this group and the most we could buy were a few meters of plastic, four rolls of seal tape, a bag of coal, gauze and a week's supply of canned food.

Now it was time to seal a room in the house. The radio advised listeners to seal a room with the least windows and the nearest to the bathroom. Whichever way we looked at it, none of the rooms in our house fitted the requirements. Like most houses in Dheisheh at the time, our house had four rooms, built with cinder blocks nearly thirty years earlier, and was filled with cracks. Furthermore, the rooms led to one another through an open courtyard, making it impossible to get to the bathroom without going outdoors.

Although it was the farthest from the bathroom, our bedroom was the only room we could seal. It was small, measuring four by three meters, and had only one window and fewer cracks in the walls than the rest of the rooms. Ahmed covered the window with plastic and secured it with seal tape. Using putty, he closed as many of the cracks in the walls as possible. Finally, he rolled up a piece of plastic over the door, which had to be secured with fresh seal tape every time the sirens went off.

After getting the room ready, we couldn't sleep in it. The air inside was too tight, and we couldn't use the kerosene heater to keep warm for fear of suffocation. There also wasn't enough space to move about since we had stored all the perishable food and several containers of water in the bedroom. It was also impossible to be inside the room and not get an eerie sense that something horrible was about to happen. It was too depressing to bear so we moved our blankets and television set into the living room, where we ate, slept, socialized, and watched TV for the next few weeks. The TV and radio were never turned off except when the electricity went off, which was quite often, and we had to operate the radio on batteries.

When the sirens went off, announcing the first scud-missile attack, I felt sedated with fear. I imagined chemical gas entering my body through my eyes, my ears and my nostrils. I imagined being the only survivor in Dheisheh. I imagined emerging from the sealed room to a dreadful stillness in the camp. I imagined going from house to house and finding everyone dead in the spot where they last sat or last lay. I realized that it would be a swift death with no visible destruction, no blown-up houses, no bent electric poles, and no gutted windows; a quiet death that destroys only the living. The hundreds of birds nesting on the gigantic pine tree down the street would die, and so would the tens of stray dogs whose howling shatters the silence of the nights. All the children who live in our neighborhood, all the babies, the girls, and the boys would die and so would Ahmed, my husband of less than a year. The thought of his death lingered.

The announcer on Radio Israel was urging people to stay calm, remain in their sealed rooms, and keep their gas masks on. He sounded solemn and frightfully serious. I don't recall how I finally managed to fall asleep that first night but I do recall waking up very early the next morning. Ahmed and my mother-in-law were both asleep. I wrapped a blanket around my shoulders and went outside. Nothing and nobody stirred. All was quiet at Saeed's house next door. I couldn't hear any of Mahmoud's eight kids moving about across the alley.

Zuhair's house, usually the noisiest in the neighborhood, was dead still. I panicked. My heart throbbed so loud that my ears hurt. I was sure, absolutely sure, that all the neighbors had suffocated to death inside their sealed rooms. I smoked one cigarette after the other, pondering what to do. I wanted to open the front gate and go check on everyone but what about the curfew?

Finally realizing that my fear of finding all my neighbors dead was far greater than my fear of being caught by an army patrol, I slipped out the door and ran to Saeed's house next door. The front gate was locked so I jumped over the wall. I knocked on the door with great urgency. The need to talk to another living soul suddenly became vital. I heard the rattling of plastic and the door opened. Saeed's mother stood there, trying to shake the sleep from her eyes.

I was never so happy to see her. We exchanged a few words and I left. I went to one more house before realizing that all the neighbors might think I was crazy walking about with my face unwashed, my hair uncombed and a huge blanket wrapped around my shoulders. I went back to the house and waited for Ahmed to wake up.

When we were placed under curfew at the outset of the war, I thought Ahmed and I would spend the entire time by ourselves. I couldn't have been more wrong. With absolutely no place to go and nothing to do for weeks on end, everyone in Dheisheh had time to socialize. Even the curfew did not stop them. Most of our neighbors and friends would come over and spend hours with us, sitting around in the living room, drinking tea with sage, watching TV and discussing the latest developments of the war. We all listened to the news round the clock. Ahmed and our neighbor, Saeed, took turns staying up all night to keep up with the latest. We would debate Saddam's next move: would he use chemical gas? How would the Allies respond if he did? We differed. The debates became heated but on one thing, we all agreed: Israel would never be the same again.

The moment the first scud hit, the Israelis panicked. They appeared on our TV screens, scared and vulnerable. It was precisely this that made us feel so euphoric. The same people who had occupied us with their guns, bombs, and iron fists were gripped with fear. We watched, with great delight, armed Israeli soldiers run out of the camp terrified. It happened every time the sirens went off. Loaded with their guns, helmets, trench coats and gas masks, they would dash out of Dheisheh to the military camp across the street. We would watch them and laugh. It was a wholehearted laughter, the kind that makes your entire body shake.

While the soldiers hid in their army camp, wearing their stupid gas masks, Dheisheh went to work. This was the best time to break the curfew and not worry about being caught. The camp's alleys would bustle with activity: two teenaged girls walk by, carting a sack of flour. An old man scurries along with an electric heater under his arm. A woman, with a big pot balanced on her head, strolls by. Two brothers carefully carry a TV set, explaining to curious onlookers that their set had broken down and they're borrowing this one from a relative. While Saddam's missiles ranged the skies, Dheisheh's refugees were busy moving things from house to house. The heavier things, the things they could not risk carrying when the soldiers were around.

Ahmed and I would stand on the roof, along with all the neighbors, and watch the scuds light the sky as they swiftly made their way to Tel Aviv. Our four rolls of seal tape had long run out and we could no longer secure the plastic on our bedroom door. Hiding in the sealed room was so very pointless.

Whenever the sirens went off, announcing the end of a missile raid, a sudden stillness would wrap Dheisheh. Not a soul, even a stray cat, would remain in sight. The soldiers were back with their guns and sticks. We would all disappear inside our houses and wait. Soon there will be another raid, another scud attack, and another risk of chemical gas making the stillness in Dheisheh eternal.

5 Diary of a Blockade (1993)

Early morning hours have been quiet in Dheisheh. Birds chirp. Pigeons coo. In the backyards, chickens stir. A pigeon flies, shifting from an almond tree to a nearby television antenna. A chicken cackles.

The mornings have been delightfully serene since Israel imposed a blockade on the West Bank more than two weeks ago. I don't hear the footsteps of laborers as they leave for work at the crack of dawn. I don't hear men coughing as they walk past my bedroom window. I don't hear doors open or slam shut. The refugee camp stays peacefully still. Nothing disturbs the silence.

But by late morning, Dheisheh is wide awake and the air is filled with noisy sounds of human activity. Drills power on and off. Hammers tear down old walls. Welding machines make a deafening screech. People call out to one another. Children play in the alleyways. Babies cry. Peddlers use their vocal cords as loudspeakers to sell cheap foam mattresses, pans and teacups. A group of youngsters follow an old peddler through our neighborhood, mimicking his every word. The weary man shoos them away, but the kids keep coming back. The peddler curses under his breath. Soon, the tormentors get bored. They laugh and go back to playing hide-and-seek.

The voice of Egyptian pop singer Warda blares from a neighbor's ghetto blaster.

"When you're near, you fill up my senses. When you're away, you fill up my senses," Warda croons.

Nida' and Ezyia, my teenage neighbors from next door, walk in and out of my house all day. First, they want to borrow a cassette tape. Then they come over to secretly smoke a cigarette they sneaked out of their father's pack. Later they drop in to ask if I want an ice cream cone from the store. Their mother marches into my house.

"Nida'! Didn't I tell you to hang the laundry hours ago?" she scolds. "And you Ezyia!" she turns to her youngest. "Your father has been waiting for 20 minutes for the newspaper he sent you to buy."

The girls make a face and leave. Half an hour later, they're back. Nida' wants nail polish remover. Ezyia wants to escape from the endless housework.

Fawzi, the neighborhood's jack-of-all trades, haggles with his friend Musa over the price of the metal window frame he is going to make for him. Fawzi shouts at his son Mohammed, "Get your lazy butt over here. I need help."

A lorry arrives and dumps a load of sand in our alley. Men and boys emerge from their houses. They help load the sand into buckets and haul it into Zuhair's house. When they're done, they stand in the sun to drink the tea with fresh mint that Zuhair's wife has made. Zuhair needs the sand to build a wall between his house and that of his neighbor, Sara. The two have been fighting and calling each other ugly names for months now. Trouble began when Sara built a window overlooking Zuhair's roof without getting his permission. To punish her, Zuhair wants to block the window by building a high barrier of cinder blocks on his roof. Now that the blockade has forced his sons and all their friends to sit at home with nothing to do, Zuhair has all the help he needs to build the wall and paint his house, too.

Meanwhile, everyone in our neighborhood is talking about Hassan. The day after the territories were sealed off, all the neighbors heard Hassan open the squeaky metal doors of his two garages. Considering that the garages had been closed for years, everyone was curious to find out what Hassan was up to.

"He's going to turn the garages into a billiard hall," Aisha says, horrified.

"What a terrific idea," smiles Ahmed. "It'll give the guys something to do."

"I'm going to tell my husband to stop him," complains Mufida. "Our neighborhood will turn into a gathering place for every young guy in the camp."

While the neighbors argue, Hassan tears down the wall separating the two garages. He brings in a pool table and the place becomes a haven for many of Dheisheh's young males. The sound of the billiard stick hitting the colored balls already has blended in with all the other sounds in our alley. But Hassan is happy. Providing food and clothing for seven children and a wife is not easy. He had a good job working as a laborer in Israel, but now, after the blockade, he needs a new source of income.

Two weeks into the blockade, our house resembles a coffee shop. With no jobs to go to, my husband Ahmed and his friends have plenty of time on their hands. They sit in the courtyard, drink black coffee, chain-smoke, and spend idle hours talking. None of them complains about the lack of money, the lack of food or the lack of things to do. Instead, they talk about the hike they want to take to a nearby mountain to collect birds' eggs. Rawhi knows just the place. He also knows some good edible plants they can collect.

Ahmed proudly tells Rawhi about the chili pepper seeds he planted in our garden that morning. "They're extra-hot," he brags.

"What about me?" protests Rawhi, "Can you give me some to plant?"

Ezyia walks in and asks Ahmed if she can borrow two decks of playing cards for her brother and his friends. A few hours later Ahmed, Rawhi and Nabieh install a bathtub in our new bathroom. They've been working on the bathroom for a week now. But no one is in a hurry.

Everyone has time. Passing away the long hours, days and nights of the blockade is an art. You have to be skillful to master it. And when you become a master, you laugh when you want to cry. You act full when you are famished. You pretend to be deaf when your kids ask for pocket money. You feign indifference when you see your refrigerator cooling nothing but a single bottle of water. And, you spend slow minutes each day pretending that you are alive, when you're not.

6   Fatima (1994)

Clutching her small black purse in her hand, Fatima makes her way down to Dheisheh's vegetable market. Although a five-minute walk from her house, it takes Fatima nearly half an hour to get there. First, she stops to greet Zuhra who sits crouched in the December sun.

"How's your health today?" asks Fatima.

"God will make it better," replies the 80-year-old woman.

Rumor in Dheisheh has it that Zuhra has the "wicked disease", a term people in Dheisheh use to describe cancer. But nobody dares confront the old woman with the question and so, her contraction of the disease remains mere hearsay.

Fatima bids Zuhra farewell and walks on. She makes a quick stop at the house of Nimeh, her relative, to say good morning. Minutes later, she is at the market. Once there, Fatima wastes no time. Her expert eyes check out the fresh produce strewn in wooden boxes on the floor. She asks Yunis, who has been running the market for years, the price of the zucchini.

"Five shekels for every three kilos," answers the old man in his old, monotone voice.

"That's too much," haggles Fatima, "can I have it for four?"

Without waiting for his answer, Fatima grabs a plastic bag, bends over the wooden box and starts picking the best-looking zucchini she can find. She tries to ignore the fact that she just cooked the green vegetable for lunch two days earlier. She tries not to think about the temper tantrum her youngest son, Majed, will throw when he finds out what's for lunch. Instead, Fatima wonders whether to stuff the zucchini with rice or stew them with potatoes, chili peppers and tomato sauce.

She weighs three kilos, places four shekels in Yunis's outstretched hand and takes another look around. The bananas look delicious and she badly wants to buy some. But at four shekels a kilo, she knows they are a delicacy she cannot afford.

Back at the house, Fatima immediately gets to work. In her efficient, yet very easy-going manner, she calls out instructions to her three daughters.

"Come bake the bread," she tells Ghadeer, 21, a pretty and very intelligent young woman who graduated from college with honors the year before.

Several months after she started her new job as a medical lab technician, Ghadeer angrily walked out on the job when the manager offered her a monthly salary of 50 dollars and expected her to work ten hours a day, six days a week. Ghadeer hates doing housework and voices several complaints before she finally settles down in front of the hot gas stove to bake the succulent bread. In contrast, Hanan, 20, is very helpful around the house and Fatima puts her in charge whenever she is away from home. For nearly six months now, Hanan has been taking a hair design course at Dheisheh's vocational training center for women and is happy to be doing something with her time.

Like her mother, Hanan is extremely beautiful. She has Fatima's round face, soft white skin, big black eyes and captivating smile. And like Fatima, who looks much younger than her 47 years, Hanan's beauty is purely natural, never touched up with any make-up whatsoever.

The youngest daughter, Ahlam, 18, is a different story altogether. She was born deaf and mute, just like her father. Fatima, who is illiterate, uses sign language of her own creation to communicate with Ahlam. Holding out the palm of one hand, Fatima brings the fingers of her other hand together and twists them in a circular motion over the open palm.

Ahlam nods, realizing that her mother wants her to do the dishes. Artistically very talented, Ahlam can look at any picture on a wall or a photo in a magazine and embroider it on a piece of a cloth. She can also sketch these pictures on her sketchpad. And even though she never went to school, Ahlam loves to place an English book on her lap and neatly copy the letters onto her note pad. She possesses an incredibly keen eye for detail. Fatima hovers over her daughters like a hen over her baby chicks. She is both a mother and a friend, maintaining a close relationship with her three daughters, as well as her three sons. Having a deaf and mute husband has forced Fatima to be in charge of every single detail around the house. A superb cook, great housewife and doting mother, she gracefully copes with the extreme hardship forced upon the family since the Israeli authorities sealed off the West Bank and Gaza Strip from East Jerusalem and Israel on March 31, 1993.

Prior to the closure nearly a year ago, Fatima's husband Mustafa, 65, sons Anwar, 23, and Issam, 19, worked as construction laborers in Israel. Together, the three earned around 750 dollars a month.

"Back then," recalls Fatima, "I used to go shopping in Bethlehem two or three times a week, spending nearly 200 shekels each time."

In those days, Fatima's kitchen was full of fresh fruits, meat and chicken and anything her children's hearty appetites desired. The girls went to Bethlehem twice a month to shop for clothes and they always had pocket money. But the closure of the territories hit the family real hard. During the first three months, the father and sons were out of work. "At the end of June, Mustafa finally managed to get an Israeli-issued permit from the Israeli civil administration that allowed him to return to his job in Israel," explains Fatima.

But her sons could not get permits to enter Israel and stayed out of work.

"Depending on the situation, including road closures, trouble with the settlers and holidays, Mustafa works an average of 20 days a month, earning about 300 dollars," remarks Fatima.

Whenever Israeli settlers block roads, preventing West Bank workers from reaching Israel, Fatima makes her husband stay at home.

"If he weren't deaf and mute, I wouldn't worry about him so much," she says. "But Mustafa can't hear gun shots, can't hear the soldiers when they order him to stop and the only way he can tell if there is a curfew is when he doesn't see any people walking about in the streets."

With the family's income slashed by more than half, Fatima has to use all her skills to keep the family from going hungry.

"I now go shopping in Bethlehem twice a month, spending no more than 37 dollars each time," she explains. "I rarely spend more than 2.5 dollars a day to buy food and even this amount isn't always available."

Ghadeer points out that the family has had to eat lentil soup for lunch for nearly a month.

"Fruits are out," she says. "It has been more than a month since we bought apples and as for bananas, we've had them only once."

Feeding a family of eight is no easy task. Fatima needs two 50-kilo sacks of flour a month, at a cost of 15 dollars per sack, to provide her family with its daily consumption of bread. And food is in addition to the phone bill, utilities, clothes, medical expenses and gifts for friends and relatives who either get married, have babies or have been in hospital.

The family has no bank account, no savings account and Mustafa's health insurance at work only covers his wife and youngest son. The family, like thousands of other Palestinian families in the territories, is forced to make do on a very low income. Perhaps what makes matters worse for Fatima is that she has spent her life savings to build a house for her eldest son Anwar. While studying English at a two-year college in Jordan, Anwar fell in love with a classmate and became engaged. After graduating with honors, he returned to the West Bank in 1992 full of hope for a bright future. After spending futile months trying to get a decent job with his college degree, Anwar started working in Israel as a construction laborer. Using Fatima's savings and borrowing the rest, the family spent 3,000 dollars in order to start building a house for Anwar above their three-room house in Dheisheh. Lack of vacant land in the camp forces all families to build vertically, thus adding to the sense of claustrophobic overcrowding in the camp. But the closure brought work on the house to a standstill. Unable to get a permit to work in Israel, Anwar borrowed some money and, in partnership with a cousin, he opened a small factory to manufacture cinder blocks. But within four months, the factory went bankrupt, putting Anwar in the red for quite a large sum.

Sometime in late 1993, Anwar started working as a laborer in the West Bank. But the 187 dollars he earns each month go to pay his debts. His new house is a skeleton. The floors need tiles. The walls need paint and all the rooms need doors and windows. Ghadeer is certain that if the family could have predicted the closure, they would not have built the house in the first place.

"My mother's savings could have at least helped us scrape by," she says.

As things stand now, Anwar's plans to marry and live in the new house have been put off indefinitely. Meanwhile, Fatima tries hard not to let all the pressure get to her. But it is not always so easy. When the children aren't around, she sits on the living-room floor near the wood stove and leans her aching head against the wall. Seconds later, the tears find their way down her rosy cheeks. She thinks about the next meal, new shoes for Ghadeer, the 50 dollars she borrowed from a neighbor and has to give back. Majed, her youngest, walks into the room and shatters her thoughts.

"Can I have some pocket money?" he asks in an uncertain voice.

Reaching inside her purse, she hands him 20 cents. It has been five days since he asked for money. Majed takes the money and as is his habit of late, he does not complain how little it is. Fatima leans her head back, closes her eyes and murmurs "God will make everything better."

7 Dheisheh Will Never Fall Again (1995)*

Mid-December 1995. Hundreds of boys pushed their fingers inside the round wiry holes and climbed up the 20-foot-high barbed fence. As the shouts and whistles of the men, women and children urged them on, the boys clung to the fence and started swinging violently. Giving way under their weight, the fence finally came tumbling down.

Young boys raced to the dozens of long metal rods which, until moments ago, held the fence in place, yanked them out of the ground, and happily dragged them home. The metal screeched against the pavement, making a horrendous and irksome sound. But the noisy and euphoric crowd was too busy celebrating the moment to really care. At long last, the half-mile-long fence that Israel's military occupation erected in mid-1987 along the main road leading to the camp was gone. Dheisheh no longer resembled a maximum-security prison.

A group of boys emerged from the crowd and rushed to the metal revolving gate, standing smack in the center of the fence. For twelve long years, the gate was Dheisheh's conduit to the world after Israel's military had sealed all the other camp entrances with unsightly stacks of concrete-filled barrels.

The boys climbed over the gate and tried to tear it down. "Get down from there," screamed the men. "The gate is going to stay."

The crowd shifted restlessly. Opinions differed. Some wanted the gate to remain; others wanted it removed. "Let's keep it as a souvenir," someone shouted. "Leave it to remind our children of the occupation's ugliness."

The crowd agreed. In the end, three years passed before someone thought of giving the souvenir gate a fresh coat of paint – this time in the green-red-black-and-white colors of the Palestinian flag. The redeployment of Israeli troops from parts of Bethlehem in December 1995 also witnessed the pullout of Israeli troops from Dheisheh. The

* (First published in *The Link* by Americans for Middle East Understanding, May–June 1999.)

camp, along with other parts of Bethlehem, was being turned over to the control of the Palestinian Authority in an area known as Zone A.

Although many were skeptical about the terms of the Oslo Accord, the redeployment nonetheless meant freedom. For the first time in many years, camp residents could walk in the streets after dark. For the first time, no one had to worry about being stopped by an army patrol and getting his or her identification papers checked. Suddenly, the notion that you could, just for the heck of it, drive to Bethlehem at midnight made grownups as happy as children being handed lollipops.

Excited by their newly found freedom, a group of boys hung a large banner over the main road leading to the camp. "Dheisheh will never fall again," it read in Arabic, English and Hebrew. Someone with a bulldozer volunteered to remove all the concrete-filled barrels blocking Dheisheh's numerous entrances as onlookers gathered to watch. Young Dheisheh men, who were once in the forefront of resisting Israel's occupation with stones, were now parading in the streets in their new Palestinian police and military uniforms. Dozens joined the Palestinian security forces. Displaying Palestinian flags had been an illegal, punishable offense, but now they fluttered proudly from rooftops and TV antennas. The taste of freedom is so sweet.

Or is it?

December 1995 was not even over when a new reality began to sink in. Happy to be rid of Israeli army patrols, Dheisheh woke up one morning to see two army jeeps, one Israeli, and one Palestinian, driving slowly along the Jerusalem–Hebron road. To their great dismay, the refugees discovered that, according to the Oslo Accord, the entire Jerusalem–Hebron road was to be under joint Israeli–Palestinian control. Once again, Dheisheh's children found reason to throw stones at the occupier. Only now, when stones are thrown at Israeli jeeps, the jeeps that go after the protesters are Palestinian.

The refugees also quickly realized that, as a result of Oslo, they were no longer free, as they had been, to go to all parts of Bethlehem. Now the district of Bethlehem was divided into three zones and Israel was still in control of the lion's share.

Reality set in. The dividing line between Zone A (under full Palestinian control) and Zone C (under full Israeli control) can be a single sidewalk or a street. Several Dheisheh residents still wanted by the Israeli authorities don't dare venture beyond concrete blocks marked gray and yellow to denote the boundary between zones. Should they cross over from one part of a street to the next, they risk being stopped and taken away by a passing Israeli army patrol. Ever so quickly, the young men who joined the Palestinian security forces and the civil service were faced with yet another harsh reality: how to make do on an income totaling around $200–$400 a month. The arrival of the Palestinian Authority brought with it an unprecedented rise in consumer prices and an unexpected rise in utility and telephone bills. How to make ends meet, pay bills on time and put a decent meal on the table has become the foremost issue on everyone's mind.

The paycheck that arrives at the end of the month is barely sufficient to last for more than one week. With no unemployment benefits and no social security, the majority of Palestinians struggle for subsistence. Indeed, if Palestinian society didn't depend on the extended family support system, it is very likely that hunger would join hands with poverty and crush people. Luckily, the extended family is still strong in Dheisheh. Married sons with children will share their meals with their parents and unmarried siblings if the family has a single income. If someone suddenly has unexpected guests and is out of coffee and doesn't have the necessary change to run to the store and buy some, they send their child next door to borrow some. If someone needs construction or renovation on their home but cannot afford paid workers, they can easily rely on cousins and friends. Helping out one another, sticking up for each other, loaning each other money, consoling each other – all beautiful, human traits that make life in Dheisheh so wonderfully bonding despite the immense hardship.

8   Where is Peace? (1996)

It is the end of 1996 and the peace we had sought for longer than we care to remember remains elusive. It was this month last year that the Israeli army redeployed from Bethlehem. Our euphoria is gone. It is gone because we realize now that the peace agreements signed between Israel and the Palestinian leadership are merely agreements that have reinforced apartheid, and made it more visible in our everyday life.

It is hard to be human and not be immensely depressed by the daily humiliation we have to endure. I am a prisoner inside Bethlehem and cannot travel anywhere. So many women around have also moved to the West Bank and don't have residency here either. We are cooped up like animals, like the ones kept in cages inside a national zoo. The difference is that we aren't animals, and living in a cage isn't for humans.

Every day in the news, we hear about Palestinian political prisoners that Israel refuses to release from its jails. Every day, we hear about settlement expansion. Every so often, we hear of another Palestinian house being demolished by the Israeli authorities. Travel to Gaza remains off-limits to so many of us. Where is peace?

I sink into depressions more often than not. But I know it is normal to feel this way when one lives in the un-normalcy of apartheid. I bet that if psychologists were to run some tests on us, they would find that we are filled with psychological scars resulting from all that we have to witness with the rise of each day.

And more and more, my depressions become so intense that I have to work hard on finding ways to prove to myself that I still have an interest in life. An interest which has dwindled to dangerous levels these past twelve months, leading me to crave death and wish it as I have not wished for something so feverishly in quite a long time. I am often surprised at my growing lack of passion for life. Nothing seems to excite me or intrigue me anymore. Rather, I am escaping inside myself, spending long hours alone, feeling melancholic, desolate and morose.

If I had the courage to end my life, I am sure I would have done so some while back. But among my many fears I have a fear of the unknown. What is on the other side? I ask myself. Is it better than what is at hand now, or is it worse? Being secular does not help of course because I have no faith in the existence of Heaven or Hell. Therefore I cannot find solace in knowing that there is an afterlife.

I do, however, believe in reincarnation. Yet how can I be reassured that in a next life, my soul will be less tortured than it is this life around? Perhaps if I could come back as the spoiled Siamese cat of some rich dame who lives on New York's Fifth Avenue, then I'd have something to look forward to. A bright red bow tied around my neck and plenty of goose liver served me in a crystal bowl by some stuffy-looking English butler.

Until then, I am here, being who I am now. I know I have no choice but to survive, to rise above the moment, to be stronger after the event and all that wonderful crap I am supposed to aspire to before death does finally come, tossing everything I have learned to the wind.

During the increasingly elusive moments when I am logical and realistic, I realize that all these gloomy feelings I am experiencing are just a phase. Nothing stands still in life and motion is what has always kept me going. I know that something will ultimately break and if it isn't I, then it will surely have to be something that will make life taste good once again. But life doesn't taste good without justice, without real freedom and real liberation.

Hence, I tell myself that I am not losing my mind. I try to convince myself that the reason I feel so close to insanity is because I am living in a country that is so self-destructive, it can derange the most rational of minds. Living in Palestine these past six years has undoubtedly been the most treacherous test of mental endurance I have ever had to withstand. Often times, I feel I would have fared better being a cactus in a blistering desert than I ever will living in this place.

Palestine, of course, needs no introduction. Everyone who has the slightest interest in world affairs knows that the Holy Land is a turbulent hotspot where peace seems to be as elusive as a cool breeze on a scorching summer afternoon. But what eludes anyone who lives outside the boundaries of Palestine is just how psychologically stagnant life here actually is. The constant political instability, the acute Israeli racism against the Palestinians, the extremely dire economic situation, the lack of human rights, the military checkpoints wherever you go and the ongoing incidents of deadly attacks and counter-deadly attacks. Life under occupation is not a life. There is absolutely nothing normal or good about it. All it does is to stagnate those who are occupied.

It is the sort of stagnation that slaughters your heart and mind, causing your senses to evaporate in the process. I can feel it happening to me. It is a slow death nibbling at me bit by tiny bit. I know I have reached the end. I can no longer watch myself wither away like this. It is too gradual and painful a death to endure.

And so I feel choked by this country. I feel as if I am a living corpse in a cemetery totally devoid of life. A living corpse waiting for something. For what? For Palestinian, Israeli and American leaders to decide the destiny of the masses who live here! Will there be ever-lasting peace? Will Jews and Arabs co-exist in the Holy Land? Will there be an independent Palestinian state? Will we have human rights? Will we have a better economy? Will we have freedom of movement? Will we have the right to live? Will Israel's occupation of us ever come to an end? Ever?

I know I want to live a life as a free woman. I want to go for a drive in my car without worrying about whether or not I have a permit to cross this or that military checkpoint. I want to go to a crowded Israeli beach and speak in Arabic without being afraid of getting dirty looks from passers-by because I'm an Arab. I want to travel abroad with my husband without wondering whether the Israelis will consider him a "security risk" thus denying him access to their airport. I want to live my life without feeling that I am a Red Indian or a nigger.

Instead, I am living in a screwed-up country where apartheid, racism and occupation is the name of the game. A country chosen by God as the spiritual cradle which influenced all three faiths of the book – Islam, Christianity and Judaism – the Holy Land should have, over the centuries, set an example to the world in how people of different faiths can live together in peace, harmony and good will.

But here we are Arabs and Jews living in an area no bigger than the American State of Vermont and we are lashing out at each other for control over the land. The Jews are oppressing the Arabs now and God knows what the state of affairs will be fifty years down the road. After all, it was fifty years ago that the Germans oppressed the Jews and look at the result. History repeats itself and the folly of man is not to learn from past injustices.

After the Oslo peace agreement was signed by the Palestinians and Israelis in September 1993, Israeli troops started pulling out of the Gaza Strip in May of the following year and then, later, from the

West Bank. A stream of light started peering at us and we thought that perhaps life would start getting better. We could not have been more wrong.

Now three years after the signing of the Oslo Accord, the situation in Palestine seems to be heading toward regional warfare and not toward a comprehensive and lasting peace. The peace agreement has divided Palestine into cantons, turning each Palestinian city into a big prison. Each city is surrounded by vastly growing Jewish settlements and Israeli confiscation of Palestinian land is at its peak. Thousands of Palestinian political prisoners are still rotting away in Israeli jails with no immediate hope for their release. The Palestinian economy is shattered and unemployment has reached alarming levels.

No one is happy and the Palestinian National Authority has done little to alleviate the situation. Nepotism is rampant and so is corruption. And, more importantly, we don't seem to be heading toward building a democratic civic society.

Oh God! Who in the world is going to look out for the rights of the little guys, the poor and uneducated who cannot survive in our world if there are no laws to protect them?

What is going to happen next, no one knows. Talk of an upcoming war is on the rise and every day I find myself growing more afraid. I am 37 years old and I cannot bear the idea of living through another war. I lived through the Arab–Israeli war of 1967 when I was 8, the Black September civil war in Jordan in 1971 when I was 12 and more recently, the Palestinian Intifada. Each of these wars has only meant death, destruction and homelessness. If there is to be another war in the region, I believe it will be far more destructive than previous wars. How do you fire back at chemical warheads? How do you shoot down nerve gas? I don't think anyone will be able to survive.

I don't want to die in a war. Who does? I'd much rather die while laughing or eating or making love. But unfortunately living in Palestine toward the end of the twentieth century means to be dead despite yourself. And if you dare dream of a better life then your dreams are shattered into pieces just like breaking glass.

9   When Time Stood Still (1996)[*]

Aisha hates the present. She doesn't care which present she's living in, she vehemently hates it. For her time stopped in the autumn of 1948 when she fled her village of Zakariya.

"Zakariya is the most beautiful place on earth," she boasts.

"They say Haifa is more beautiful," someone teases.

"Haifa my foot," she retorts.

"I'm telling you Zakariya is the best. We had olive trees and fig trees as far as the eye could see. We grew the best tomatoes too. They were big and juicy and I've yet to taste any tomatoes like them."

Once on the subject of Zakariya, nothing can stop Aisha. Most of the time she doesn't even care if anyone is listening. It is as if she enters a trance and is transformed through time. She keeps on talking.

"We had an abundant harvest of tomatoes each summer. We couldn't eat them all and that is why we stored them for winter. We would slice them, sprinkle salt on them, and put them in the sun to dry. Come winter, we would soak them in water and have fresh tomatoes to eat. Almighty God, damn the Israelis and the day we set eyes on them," she sighs.

A single tear gently rolls down Aisha's wrinkled cheek. She wipes it quickly before anyone takes notice. Those who know her well know she is thinking about her son Mohammed.

"He was still sucking milk from my breast when we left Zakariya. He wouldn't stop crying. He cried the entire time that we hid in the hills surrounding Zakariya. When we heard that the Jews had entered our village and started our long walk toward Hebron to the southeast, he still continued to cry. Then one day he stopped. I thought he was tired and had gone to sleep. When we stopped for the night and I uncovered my breast to feed him, he did not stir. I carried his listless body in my arms for four days before we finally reached a village in the outskirts of Hebron and his father dug a hole in the grounds of the local cemetery and buried him."

Of the nine children that Aisha bore, only five survived. The rest died sometime in the 1950s when Aisha found herself living in a

* (First published as an article in *Palestine Report*, May 1, 1998.)

small tent in what became known as Dheisheh Refugee Camp just outside Bethlehem. An only daughter, who was terribly spoiled by her parents, Aisha was not accustomed to the hardship that was to come. "We came to Dheisheh with nothing except the clothes on our backs. We had no money at all and Abdul Fatah had had to sell our camel in Hebron so we could buy food for the children."

Aisha married Abdul Fatah when she was 13. "I was a little girl and had no idea what marriage was about. Because I was their only daughter, my parents did not force me to do any housework and I was always out in the barley fields playing with my girlfriends. After the wedding, I lived with my parents-in-law until it was time for me to bathe," she murmurs.

"You mean you never took a bath before your wedding?" Aisha's young granddaughter asks shyly.

"No silly, I am talking about taking my first bath when my first menstrual cycle ended. When I married your grandfather, I wasn't menstruating yet and had to live with his parents for three months until I did. After the first cycle ended and I washed myself, I moved into my husband's house to consummate the marriage."

Aisha never loved Abdul Fatah. She never forgave him for marrying her at such a tender age. Till today, she insists that he was 36 years old when they married.

"How could he have been 36 when he died at the age of 88 in 1984, mother?" her son Mahmoud shouts angrily.

"He was 26 when he married you." But Aisha refuses to listen. "He was an old man and had no business marrying a young child like me," she insists.

Aisha's resentment of Abdul Fatah is not uncharacteristic of her. She hates everything in her life. She hates being a refugee, she hates the Jordanians for ruling the West Bank, and she hates the Israelis and their occupation. She hates everything that happened to her after that fateful autumn in 1948 and no one could say anything or do anything to make her change her mind. For her time came to a standstill when she walked out of Zakariya and it will never go into motion again until she can go back.

"I insist on my right of return and will never accept compensation instead," Aisha says feverishly. "I want to go back to my land."

And Aisha knows exactly where her land is. She keeps all the yellowish and tattered land deeds inside a small tin container. Dated back to the 1930s, each land deed specifies the boundaries of each piece of land that Abdul Fatah owned.

"Read this and see for yourself," says Aisha as she unfolds one of the land deeds and sticks it in her grandson's face. The boy laughs.

"But Grandmother, Zakariya doesn't look the same anymore. How can you tell where your land is?" The boy reads out loud. "Witnesses signing this document testify that Abdul Fatah bought a piece of land on this date. The land is located between Saleh's and Salman's wheat fields. Saleh's fig trees mark the land's northern boundary while Salman's well marks the southern boundary."

The boy tries to explain to his grandmother that Zakariya has been transformed in the past fifty years and that it is impossible to identify the family's property. Aisha angrily snatches the deed out of his hand and puts it away.

"I know exactly where the land is," she screams at him. "All they have to do is take me there and I'll show them. I haven't gone senile yet."

Aisha shoos the grandchildren out of the room. "They think I'm going to give it up just like that," she mumbles out loud. "For fifty years I have held onto these deeds and they think I'm going to give it up."

Then almost in wail, she starts. "I had to walk for miles on end to gather wood and sell it for peanuts in order to feed my children. They think it is easy being a refugee. I didn't ask to be a refugee. I didn't ask to live with thousands of other people in one and a half damn square kilometers. There is no air to breathe here in Dheisheh. All the air is in Zakariya. We had a nice breeze even on the hottest of days."

Just as suddenly as she starts talking, Aisha stops. Minutes later, everyone in the house can hear her cry. It is a muffled and choked sound.

"Stop Grandmother," begs her granddaughter. "I swear to God Almighty that we'll go back. We are from Zakariya and we must go back."

Aisha doesn't answer and the girl knows better than to push her luck. As the children go outside to play, Aisha starts singing a sad melody, making up the words as she goes.

"Oh my son Mohammed where are you? Why don't you come and see what has become of me? Oh my son Mohammed if only you were here. You would be a grown man now and maybe an engineer. Oh my son Mohammed, I held you in my arms. My milk was waiting for you but may God forgive you, you did not open your eyes."

10 The French Connection (1997)*

Until seven years ago, the 14,000 inhabitants of Montataire, a French city located in the district of L'Oise 60 kilometers north of Paris, had never heard of Dheisheh Refugee Camp in Bethlehem. Likewise, the 9,000 residents of Dheisheh had never heard of Montataire. But in 1990 all that changed following the signing of a twin-city agreement between the municipality of Montataire and Dheisheh. "The agreement was unique in that it marked the first such twinning between a city and a Palestinian refugee camp," says Dheisheh resident Wajieh el-Sheik, Director of the Education and Training Unit at the Democracy and Workers Rights Center, who signed the memorandum of the agreement.

Following the twinning, the names Dheisheh and Palestine, along with the Palestinian flag, have been added beside the word "Montataire" on the large signboard at the entrance of the city and Montatairians have been making many friends in Dheisheh. So far, six delegations from Dheisheh have visited Montataire including a football team, which played three games with their French counterparts in the summer of 1996, winning all games, and returning home with a trophy.

"Our main worry was how to play, for the first time, on a football field laid with grass after being used to playing on dusty fields filled with pebbles," recalls Ra'ed Shabaan, 29, one of the team players. "That's why winning the cup was such a great achievement for us."

Until their trip to Montataire, most team members had never left the West Bank, let alone been on an airplane. "Our trip really started when we crossed the Allenby Bridge into Jordan to catch the flight for Paris," says team member Hazem Qasas, 19. "I can honestly say that our ten-day stay in Montataire was the highlight of my life."

In August 1996, a group of eleven high school and college students from Montataire visited Dheisheh for twelve days, staying with families in the camp. They were the seventh delegation to visit Dheisheh.

* (First published in *Palestine Report*, December 19, 1997.)

"Even though we do not speak each other's language, we were somehow able to communicate," says Ra'ed Sudqi, 20, who hosted one of the French female students in his home. "The French were surprised by our hospitality and we admired their interest in getting to know all about life in our camp."

In addition to exchanging delegations, the Montataire–Dheisheh twin-city agreement also includes an ambitious plan to renew the electric network in the camp. "Most of the equipment is already at a port in France waiting to be shipped to us," says Ahmed Muhaisen, Twin-City Committee President and Director of the Department of Twin-Cities and NGOs at the Department of Refugee Affairs in the PLO.

"We sent two Dheisheh residents who work as technicians at the Jerusalem Electric Company on a training course in Montataire earlier this year so they can carry out the work when the equipment arrives," adds Muhaisen. Furthermore, Dheisheh is about to receive a fire truck from Montataire and a water pump to help solve the problem of water distribution to high areas in the camp.

Based on the Montataire–Dheisheh experience, the French and Palestinians decided to form the Association of Twin-City Committees between French Cities and Palestinian Refugee Camps in order to achieve similar twin-city agreements. Jointly headed by Montataire resident Fernand Tuil, Secretary of the Communist Party in L'Oise and Muhaisen, the Association was formed in 1996, and has quickly gone to work. A delegation headed by Muhaisen and including Palestinian legislation Dalal Salameh of Balata Refugee Camp, and Dr. Jawad Tiebi of Khan Younis Refugee Camp, went to France last November to sign nine more agreements between French cities and Palestinian refugee camps. The refugee camps include four camps in the West Bank, four in the Gaza Strip and one in Jerusalem. The West Bank refugee camps and their twin cities are: Arroub in Hebron and Saint Maximin; Balata in Nablus and Saint Ouen; Askar in Nablus and Mers Les Bains; Far'a in Nablus and Longueil-Annel; Jalazone in Ramallah and Chambly. The refugee camps in Gaza and their twin cities are Bureij and Mouy; Deir el-Balah and Saint Leu; Khan Younis and Evry; Maghazi and Villers Saint Paul; as well as Shufat in Jerusalem and Thourotte.

"We are currently negotiating with eight municipalities in southern France who are interested in signing twin-city agreements," says Muhaisen. "The French are keen on expanding the agreements to include more refugee camps in the West Bank and Gaza as well as the refugee camps in Lebanon."

"In the next year or two, we hope to twin all 59 refugee camps in the West Bank, the Gaza Strip, Lebanon, Syria and Jordan," says Fernand Tuil. "The international community knows nothing about the refugee camps and since there can be no peace in Palestine without the refugee camps, the international community must learn about these camps. The twinning agreements are by far the best way to educate people about the camps."

According to Palestinian legislator Dalal Salameh, the twinning agreements indicate that there are political parties in these French municipalities that are highly aware of the Palestinian cause and the suffering of the Palestinian people. "The French are eager to establish direct contact in order to learn more and get to the truth, especially since we live in an important spot in the world and have a cause which has lasted for a considerable period of time," she says.

A 30-member delegation, including the ten mayors who already signed twin-city agreements with the camps and mayors who are interested in signing agreements, are expected to visit the refugee camps of the West Bank and Gaza Strip next March.

"When these mayors come and see the reality in Palestine, they will go back to France and tell others about it," says Tuil. The delegation plans to hold a press conference in Montataire, prior to its departure for Palestine to talk about the twin-city agreement and a similar conference is planned after the delegation arrives in Dheisheh.

"We want to intensify these field trips in the short term in order to provide the French with a close look at the refugee problem and get support for the existing refugee institutions which provide services to the residents of the camps," explains Salameh. "There is obviously a severe reduction in the services that UNRWA [United Nations Relief & Works Agency] is providing, particularly to women, children and the handicapped." Salameh hopes that the twinning relations will bring about the much needed political pressure on the French government to fulfill its obligations to UNRWA, which is suffering from a severe budget deficit. "We are asking our French friends to pressure their political parties, and hence their government, to fulfill its commitments to UNRWA."

As to the basis on which the refugee camps that were twinned were chosen, Salameh explains that the refugee camps do not differ one from the other. "It is the same cause whether the camp is in the West Bank or Lebanon. We did, however, try to take into consideration choosing camps from various geographical locations in order to recruit all the skills and capabilities for the benefit of the refugee cause."

11 The Glory of the Intifada (1997)*

When the Palestinian Intifada erupted in the West Bank and Gaza Strip on December 9, 1987, Nidal, then 19, was finishing his senior year in high school.

"I had just been released from an Israeli jail and was taking special classes to make up for lost time in school," he recalls.

Now, in 1997, Nidal is a sophomore at Bethlehem University, majoring in social studies. Like so many other Palestinians his age, he was unable to complete his education during the Intifada. Instead, he was actively resisting the occupation, was on Israel's wanted list twice, and spent a total of three years in Israeli jails.

"I was 14 the first time I went to prison in 1984," he says. "Altogether, I was jailed 13 different times and was wanted by the Israelis, first for one year and then for six months."

The last time Nidal was released from prison was in January 1996, one month after the Palestinian Authority took over control of Bethlehem.

"It was my most difficult time in prison," he remembers. "I spent 50 straight days under interrogation and then I was placed under administrative detention for six months."

Nidal's twin brother, Ra'fat shares a similar background. He was arrested 13 times, starting at the age of 14, and spent a total of three years in Israeli prisons. Ra'fat and his younger brother Hazem, 23, are still wanted by the Israelis and have not been able to leave Zone A (under total Palestinian control) of Bethlehem since December 1995.

"The Israelis claim we were involved in shooting incidents, carried out by the Popular Front for the Liberation of Palestine (PFLP) against Israeli targets, and they have repeatedly asked the Palestinian Authority to arrest us and turn us over," he says.

Indeed, Ra'fat and Hazem were arrested twice by the Palestinian Authority.

"The first time was 15 days after the Palestinians took over control of parts of the Palestinian territories and the second time was in

* (First published in *Palestine Report*, December 10, 1997.)

1996," explains Ra'fat. "The Palestinian Authority said that our arrest was for our own protection but we went on a hunger strike for 24 days and following public protest, we were taken out of jail and placed under house arrest for one month. They insisted that we stay in a house in the town of Beit Sahour rather than remain in our house in Dheisheh."

Ra'fat, married and the father of two, has not been able to get a decent job for well over a year.

"I can't leave Zone A in Bethlehem for fear of arrest by the Israelis and I lost my job at a Bethlehem gas station following my arrest by the Palestinian Authority."

Ra'fat occasionally helps his father in his carpentry shop until something better comes along.

"Nowadays, I sit around and recall the beauty of the Intifada," he says fondly. "I remember the days when we were wanted by the Israelis and how we fought together against a common enemy. We felt that we were making a step forward, no matter how small, toward a greater goal."

"I remember the days when there were curfews and we would sneak in food supplies and distribute them to camp residents," says Nidal.

"There were also the times when we were wanted by the Israelis and would spend our nights moving from house to house, never getting any sleep or staying in one place for long. Even though things were tough, the morale of the people was so strong and everyone had such high hopes."

Nidal's wife, Manal, 23, was only 13 when the Intifada erupted but she has fond memories of it as well.

"I miss those days a lot. They were the most beautiful days of my life. True, everyone was scared of the soldiers and their guns but we had dignity and it was our dignity that made us so defiant."

Manal was shot in the chest by a live bullet during a demonstration in Dheisheh in 1989. She was 15 at the time and until today, she suffers from pain in her lungs and occasionally has difficulty breathing. Her injury, however, does not seem to bother her. Instead, she is more concerned about the depressed mood of the Palestinians today.

"We never felt depressed before or during the Intifada," she says excitedly. "People stuck together and when someone was shot, everyone would race to rescue them. They were great days."

As if to emphasize his wife's feelings, Nidal adds reflectively, "The Intifada made us feel so equal to the Israelis. The mood of the people was so elated. Children in Dheisheh, some as young as five, would walk to al-Maqassed Hospital in Jerusalem to visit the wounded and donate blood. Even the children wanted to do their share."

Although the Abu Aker family speak fondly of the days of the Intifada, they still have not forgotten the pain or the loss. Nidal's brother, Mohammed was shot by Israeli soldiers in August 1988, and died of his wounds in October 1990. Were he still alive, Mohammed would have turned 25 this year. Hazem, meanwhile, has lost vision in his right eye after he was shot with a rubber-coated metal bullet in 1990. "Losing my brother makes me real sad but I also realize that the road of struggle is not an easy one and it comes at a high price," says Nidal. "If I want to regard matters from a personal point of view, away from politics, I might think in terms of regret and if I measure matters through gain and loss, then it has been a loss. However, from a political viewpoint, what we went through during the Intifada was a sacrifice and a duty. I don't regret it because struggle and sacrifice is the right direction for our people."

Nidal believes that the refugees played a very important and active role in the Intifada – which started in Jabalya Refugee Camp in Gaza and then Balata Refugee Camp in the West Bank. "The refugees were harmed the most as a result of the occupation. They were the ones who lost their land and became refugees. This is why the refugees insist on their right of return and will not settle for anything less."

12   Where Do We Belong? (1997)

"My daughter is getting married," Halimeh tells her neighbor Amneh.

"Congratulations. "Who is the groom?" Amneh asks.

"He's Hassan's son. You know him. He's from our village. Hassan was good friends with my father back in Zakariya. He was a decent and well-liked man."

Halimeh means, of course, that Hassan and her father were good friends before 1948, when the two were still young men living in the village of Zakariya, northwest of Hebron, which was destroyed by Israel after the 1948 War. The fact that Hassan's son is marrying her daughter makes Halimeh very happy.

"My eldest daughter married a stranger from another village and I'm so glad that my youngest is marrying one of us. It puts me more at ease."

Although Halimeh has lived in Dheisheh Refugee Camp these past fifty years, she still identifies herself as a Zakariyan. This is just how it is. You sense her identification with Zakariya in all the stories she tells you.

"During the occupation, I worked as a cleaning woman in the dormitories of Hebrew University in Jerusalem. About seven other women from Dheisheh worked with me. We were all from Zakariya except for Sheikha. She was from Faloujeh (northeast of Gaza). Oh yes! I forgot about Mariam. She was from Beit Nateef (near Zakariya). Nice woman."

Although Dheisheh's refugees come from more than forty Palestinian villages in pre-1948 Palestine, they all still identify themselves with their villages in more ways than one. The refugees of Zakariya, who make up the majority of the refugees in Dheisheh, live in the same vicinity in the camp. Theirs is known as Zakarweh neighborhood. In fact, since there are no street names in Dheisheh, each neighborhood is named after the village where its residents come from. There is the Ajajreh neighborhood, in reference to the village of Ajour (northwest of Hebron); the Walajieh neighborhood, in reference to the village of Walajeh (northwest of Bethlehem). The list goes on.

Until today, residents of the same village maintain close ties. If a Dheisheh refugee from the village of Walajeh dies, all the Dheisheh clans from his village go to pay their respects. If a man from Ajour accidentally hits someone with his car, the clan elders from Ajour go visit the victim's family to make amends. If two men from different villages get into a fight and injure one another, clan elders from both villages meet to make peace between the two. The examples are numerous.

"The experience of the 1948 Catastrophe was devastating for people," explains Abdullah, an elderly man from the village of Beit Eitab. "When we came to Dheisheh, it was only natural for us to stick together and help each other out. Besides, we have customs and traditions and the Catastrophe didn't take those away. We still go about our social duties in the same manner that we did back home."

But fifty years is almost a lifetime and there are now third- and fourth-generation refugees born in the camp. Can a second- or third-generation refugee, born and raised in Dheisheh, have the same ties to his village as his elders?

Nader doesn't think so. "Why can't we be realistic for a change?" he says heatedly. "I don't feel the same about Zakariya as my father does."

Nader says he has been visiting Zakariya with his parents ever since he was a child. "The first time I went there, I was astounded by how beautiful the area is. I looked at the peak of a hill and imagined building a house for myself there. But, it was a very brief and momentary dream. When I looked around and saw the Israeli houses built on Zakariya's land, the roads and the schools, I said to myself: who are we fooling, this doesn't belong to us anymore."

Nader is getting irritated and angry. He is having a heated discussion with friends about their ties to their villages.

"Let me ask you something," he says scornfully. "What do we know about our villages? Other than the stories we hear our parents tell us, what information do we really have about our villages?"

Everyone agrees that all they know is what their parents tell them.

"Did you ever read about your village in books, to try and educate yourselves?"

No one answers. "Well then," reflects Nader, "don't you find it odd that we live in close proximity to Zakariya and yet we are ignorant about it? I mean, for God's sake, it is not as if we have moved to Japan. Zakariya is only miles away from Dheisheh and what do we know about it, other than it being our village?"

Indeed, why don't refugees like Nader know more about the places they call home? Nader contends the reason is ignorance.

"Our parents were ignorant. Why didn't they teach us about our villages when we were children? If they had, our ties to the villages would certainly be stronger than they are today."

Nader's cousin Yousef disagrees. "My father told me a lot about Zakariya and this is why, unlike you, I feel closely connected to it."

"Yes but in your heart, do you believe you are going to return to it?" asks Nader.

Yousef grins sardonically. "In my heart I believe that it is either us or them. I don't see that we can both be here on this land. It won't work. It is a struggle to the end, either them or us. I don't accept the fact that my father used to own land in Zakariya when here I am, only owning the house I live in in Dheisheh so that an Iraqi Jew, just because he is a Jew, can come live on my father's land."

Everyone in the room falls silent, immersed in their own thoughts. They're thinking of what their lives would be like if they still lived in their villages.

"My parents always tell me stories about their life in Zakariya before 1948," says Nader. "Sometimes when my father is going on and on about it, I ask him: 'Did you see the Jews?' He tells me he hadn't. I ask him again: 'When you fled the village in the autumn of 1948, did you see any Jews?' My father still says no. So I ask him: 'Why then did you leave? Why the hell did you leave?'"

Now it is Yousef's turn to be irritated and angry.

"All right, so people were ignorant. They were afraid for their lives. They heard about the Deir Yassin massacre and other massacres and they were afraid they'd be butchered as well. Besides, what sort of weapons did they have to defend themselves against the armed Jews and their British supporters?"

"They could have at least tried," says Nader with a pained look on his face.

Yousef's father tried. He fought in several battles in 1948 and lived to talk about it.

"The Palestinians had no weapons worth mentioning; they were not organized and did not have a central command. They had no chance," argues Yousef. "This is why I say, it is either us or them. There is no room for both."

The front door opens and Nader's 9-year-old cousin walks in.

"We're off school tomorrow and the day after," she blurts excitedly.

"How come?" asks Nader.

"They have two marches to commemorate the anniversary of the Catastrophe. The children are going to carry keys to their old houses in the villages and go on a march."

Everyone in the room smiles at the girl who is happily waving a small Palestinian flag in her hand.

"The teacher told us to hang a flag on our front gate," says the girl. "She also said to hang a black flag because of the Catastrophe but I don't have a piece of black cloth."

"I'll find you one," offers Nader's wife.

The girl jumps with joy and everyone laughs.

Then the girl innocently asks, "What is this Catastrophe thing? What does it mean?"

Everyone is too shocked to speak. Moments later, Nader asks, "Didn't your teacher explain to you why you are going on the march?"

The girl shakes her head. "The Catastrophe is when the Jews came and occupied Palestine and ..." Nader proceeds to explain. Issa shifts in his seat. Throughout the discussion, he did not say a word. Now he looks at everyone and grins.

"There you have it all over again. Ignorance!"

13 Remembering Our Dead (1997)*

A monument stands high at one of the main entrances to Dheisheh Refugee Camp. An oblong stone structure resembling the pre-1948 map of Palestine, the eye-catching monument was built in 1997 by the Dheisheh Society of Martyr Families to honor the more than 15 camp residents who were killed during decades of occupation. The monument is there to remember them all, starting with Abdullah Tayieh, a high-school student killed in 1956 by Jordanian troops during an anti-Baghdad Pact protest in Bethlehem, and ending with Ali Sajadi, a high-school dropout killed in 1993 while handling an explosive device left behind by Israeli soldiers.

A small patch of land surrounding the monument was supposed to be turned into a much needed public park for camp residents, but funding to complete the project never came through. This is hardly unusual in today's Palestinian Territories, where funds are hard to come by to improve the lot of the living, let alone honor the memory of the dead.

While the monument stands high as a constant reminder of those who sacrificed their lives for freedom and independence, it is nonetheless a sad symbol of the state of Palestinian affairs today. The names of Dheisheh's martyrs are not engraved on the monument and not a single tree, or rose bush or decorative plant fills the desolate space around it. The sidewalk and steps leading to the monument are filled with twisted metal rods, discarded wood planks, litter, and other construction debris left behind by someone who recently built a nearby garage. Lack of funds, the failure of UNRWA to provide the camp with sufficient sanitary services, and the indifference of camp residents are the reasons why Dheisheh's only public monument screams out for tender attention.

But although Dheisheh's refugees seem to lack initiative in maintaining and beautifying the monument park, there is hardly a refugee, young or old, who doesn't remember the names of the camp's victims and even the year of their untimely deaths. Nida',

---

* (First published in *The Link* by Americans for Middle East Understanding, May–June 1999.)

24, looks astonished if someone compliments her for reciting the
names. For her, knowing the names of those who died is one of these
things in life that she must know, has to know. "They were our
martyrs," she states indignantly. Like so many other young people
her age, Nida' cannot forget the pain-ridden years of the Intifada
even if she wants to. During that fateful year of 1989 when a record-
high six young refugees were shot dead in the camp by Israeli
soldiers, Nida', then 14, was herself shot in the abdomen. It
happened during a demonstration commemorating the end of 40
days of mourning following the shooting death of Roufaida Abu
Laban, Dheisheh's only female Intifada victim. Roufaida was shot
between the eyes by an Israeli sniper on April 17, 1989. Before being
shot and falling to the ground, Nida' witnessed the shooting of
several other young people that day. Her description of the events,
the blood, the ensuing chaos is as crystal-clear as though she were
describing something that happened just last night. It could be
because she occasionally suffers recurring pains from her old injury
that makes it so hard for her to forget. But it also could be because
she named her daughter Roufaida in honor of her sister-in-law, who
didn't live to see her brother Ahmed marry Nida' in 1993. It is hard
to say. Whatever the reason, Nida' never fails to surprise anyone.
Out of the blue, she'll blurt out something like, "If Roufaida were
alive, she would have finished college by now." Going on as if she
were talking to herself, she'll say, "But if she were married, she would
have children. I wonder how many she would have had by now?" As
abruptly as she had started speaking, Nida' falls silent, her thoughts
trail off, and she quickly wipes the tears that begin to spring from her
eyes. Life always manages to go on for the living.

Israeli soldiers killed ten Dheisheh refugees during the Intifada,
including one who was killed while handling an explosive device.
Eight of those killed were 19 years of age or younger. But the
youngest of all was Bassam Ghrouze who, at the tender age of 12,
was shot by an Israeli sniper one cold February in 1991. In April 1998,
as part of the activities to commemorate 50 years of the Palestinian
Catastrophe, students at the Dheisheh UNRWA School for Boys were
asked to write about their lives. Several of their accounts have been
translated into English and placed on the newly established
Dheisheh camp website. One of these accounts is a moving essay by
seventh-grader Mutasem Ghrouze about his deceased brother:

Although it has been seven years, I am still sad whenever I
remember my brother Bassam. His martyrdom is still fresh in our

minds. Bassam was very special and our love for him is deeply engraved in our hearts. He was an energetic, creative and well-mannered child. He acted older than his age and was quite bold. But in one depressing moment, he was gone. He was shot dead by an Israeli soldier. The soldier's heart was filled with hate and resentment. The soldiers had neither value for human life nor any value for a child's life. Bassam was martyred on a Sunday. I will always think of that day as a very black day because it left our hearts heavy with sorrow that will stay with us as long as we live. Yes, Bassam was shot dead on a Sunday. It was February 10, 1991. The sun was almost setting. The sunset took Bassam with it. He never came back home and he never will. But even though he is gone, his memory will live with us for eternity.

In addition to Mutasem, Fida, 14, writes about her father who spent 27 months in an Israeli prison, held there without charge or trial. Ala', 12, writes about the time he was beaten on the way home from school by an Israeli soldier while Mahmoud, 12, writes how he was dragged by his arm across the floor, when an army patrol stormed his family home. Malek, 12, tells of the time he was caught outside his house during a curfew, and how the soldiers brought him home, beat his father, then went to his father's falafel shop, soaked his money in frying oil, and stole provisions with which he made his living. Mahmoud, 13, happily recounts the time the soldiers couldn't catch him, because "I was faster than them." And Ihab, 12, writes how his two uncles were forced to stand under a water drainage pipe, in freezing winter weather.

These are the children of Dheisheh at the turn of the millennium.

14   Where Did Santa Go? (1998)*

The year must have been 1965, or maybe it was 1966. I don't quite remember. What I do remember is that it was Christmas time and my maternal grandparents' house on the Mount of Olives in Jerusalem was bustling with exciting pre-holiday activity.

Grandma Marie was in her large kitchen baking gingerbread cookies. The aromatic smell of ginger and nutmeg seeped through the house as she pulled one tray of succulent cookies after the other out of the hot oven. Grandpa Attallah, meanwhile, was busy decorating the tall, pine Christmas tree. By the time he was done, we had the most enchanting Christmas tree I had ever seen.

On Christmas Eve, Grandma prepared a feast for us. Afterwards, we gathered in the warm living room where Grandpa played the piano and we sang Christmas carols. I remember standing next to the piano, as was always my habit, and watching Grandpa's dark long fingers, with the many brown spots, easily glide across the black and white keys. It was one of those rare times in my childhood, and even in my adult life, when I have felt completely safe, loved, and happy.

Now the year is 1998 and I'm spending another Christmas in Dheisheh, an eye-blink away from the manger where Christ was born. A small, artificial Christmas tree stands on a corner table in my living room, looking lifeless, unattended and out of place. I don't even bother turning on its colorful lights at night. Somehow, there isn't much to celebrate this year.

Hunger strikes and demonstrations to demand the release of the more than 3,000 Palestinian prisoners from Israeli jails have been in the headlines for most of December. Then came the joint U.S.–U.K. air strikes against Iraq, the sickening way in which the West has tried to justify its slaughter of human life, and the revolting acquiescence of most Arab governments to the whole affair.

And if all this isn't enough to put a damper on our holiday spirit, the Palestinian Authority has done its share. For one week in mid-December, it closed six local TV stations and a radio station, and

---

* (First published in *The Link* by Americans for Middle East Understanding, May–June 1999.)

arrested nine Palestinian journalists. Their crime: covering anti-U.S. demonstrations, which spread in the Palestinian Territories following air strikes against Iraq.

On Christmas Day, and with very little to feel joyful about, I go visit my next-door neighbor. Time spent with her six wonderful children might be the remedy to ease my pain. I walk in and find the kids watching live TV coverage of the Christmas parade in Bethlehem.

"You guys don't know anything about Christmas!" I tease.

"Oh yes we do," blurts 8-year-old Maram. "It is when Santa Claus wears his funny red suit and goes around giving gifts and candy to children."

"No, stupid, he has a funny white beard, not a funny red suit," 9-year-old Khloud adds quickly.

"He is fat," giggles 6-year-old Rana.

"How do you know what Santa looks like?" I ask.

"We see him on TV. He has a big bag full of gifts and he gives them to the children," volunteers 10-year-old Malak.

"Aunt Muna, how come Santa does not come to our house?" Maram asks unexpectedly.

I stare at her.

"You don't know anything," Malak answers. "He only visits the Christians and we are not Christian, isn't that right Aunt Muna?"

All eyes turn to me, waiting for the intelligent answer of an adult. "Well, this is true but many Muslims put a Christmas tree in their homes and join the celebrations in Bethlehem. Christmas is a holiday for everyone," I explain.

"So how come Daddy does not take us to Bethlehem?" asks 4-year-old Zuzu.

Before I have time to think of an answer, Khloud throws her small arms in the air and says, exasperated, "Because silly, if we go, Daddy will have to buy all of us toys and sandwiches and soft drinks. It will cost a lot of money."

Everyone is quiet, as if trying to make sense of what Khloud just said. "The Christians are so lucky," concludes Maram.

I open my mouth to speak when suddenly a popular video clip of an Egyptian song starts on TV. Maram races for the remote control and turns up the volume. The girls start to dance, forgetting all about Santa Claus and Christmas.

As their giggles fill the room, I get up to leave. The girls run to me, clinging to my arms and waist. "Please stay and have breakfast with us," they all scream. I smile and ask what they'd like me to bring them for breakfast. "It doesn't matter, Aunt Muna, just say you'll come," they all shout. I smile at them and tell them that nothing in the world would make me miss breakfast with them. And nothing ever does.

Nearly 60% of Dheisheh's population are children under the age of 16. With the exception of a handful of children whose parents can afford to send them to expensive private schools in Bethlehem, the children attend classes in the two Dheisheh schools run by UNRWA. When they finish the ninth grade, the children then have to transfer to public schools outside the camp. Overcrowding in the camp's schools requires the student body to be split into two shifts, one in the morning and one in the afternoon; even with that, class sizes exceed thirty. A single cultural center in Dheisheh provides some children with activities, but hardly enough to cover the need. With no extra-curricular activities to occupy their time or broaden their horizons, the majority of the children spend their free time playing in the camp's alleys. There are no public parks and no playgrounds to keep them off the streets, and the dire economic conditions of their parents also means that very few have toys at home.

Although Bethlehem is very near, most children only see the city when they go with their mothers when it is time to shop for clothing. Most have never been to Jerusalem. Outings or picnics are as rare as a cool breeze on a hot summer's day.

Of course, the children are too young to fathom military closures or to really comprehend poverty. Instead, they are a vivacious lot, very bright and certainly capable of looking out for themselves at a very tender age. The camp is their safe haven, and in its streets and alleys they quickly learn how to dodge approaching cars, how to defend themselves against older and meaner kids, and how to coax their parents into handing over the change they bring back from the store. It is the survival of the fittest at work.

In the ten years I've lived in Dheisheh, I don't recall seeing a child who is a sissy or a cry-baby. On many a winter's day, I've watched the kids next door walk by themselves to the camp's medical clinic to get treated for the flu and then watched them run home with medicines in hand. On occasion I would ask the kids to fetch me hot bread from a nearby bakery, only to hear them say that the bakery had just closed for renovations.

"How do you know?" I always find myself asking, only to get the usual answer – "We know everything."

15 Male vs. Female Honor (1998)[*]

It was getting late and no one was left at the wake in Dheisheh except the women related to the deceased. They sat on the floor foam mattresses in the big family room and waited for their husbands to come and take them home. With no strangers around, the women, all from the camp, and ranging in age from 14 to 70, moved from one topic to the next, talking and gossiping about anything and everything.

"Did you hear what happened to the woman from Artas[1] yesterday?" asked Na'imeh, a 43-year-old mother of seven. "She was shot dead by her cousins who found out she was having an affair. They killed her lover too."

"I've seen her once or twice before," remarked Mariam. "Wasn't she married and a mother of five?"

"Yes," replied Na'imeh. "Her lover was also married and a father of three. After shooting the woman, her relatives came to his house, told him they needed to have a word with him and riddled his body with 18 bullets. They are from the Ta'amreh tribe and I think they live in the village of Za'tara.[2] They are very tough when it comes to matters of family honor."

"Shooting this bad woman isn't a good enough punishment for her," commented Safa.

"They should have cut her into tiny pieces and made her watch herself die a slow death. This should be the punishment of an adulteress."

"What a terrible woman," said Yusra in disgust. "She had a husband providing her with food and shelter. What else did she need? She deserves to die for not honoring the man who put food on her table."

The discussion went on and on. I sat there and listened as almost every woman in the room spoke her mind. To my disbelief, all were in support of this "honor" killing, regarding it as the only logical

[*] (First published in *Palestine Report*, June 5, 1998.)
[1] A small village next to Dheisheh.
[2] A small Bedouin village east of Bethlehem.

punishment for women who commit the ultimate sin. By taking this stand, none of the women brought up the issue of evidence and none, of course, regarded murder as a severe form of punishment for a sin of the flesh. Perhaps what is unusual in this most recent "honor" killing is that the man involved was also killed. Usually, these killings involve only women. In fact, one never hears of a man who was killed because he dishonored his family. The double standards are immense. A married man not only can have an extra-marital affair and get away with it, he can, if he chooses to, marry the woman and end up with a second wife. His behavior does not appear to dishonor anyone in his family and he certainly won't lose his life because of it. According to the law, if a woman catches her husband with another woman and kills him, she can be sentenced to death whereas if a man catches his wife with another man and kills her, it is considered an "honor" killing and he may be sentenced to two years in prison. In fact, the double standards are so extreme, that a man can go home to his wife and tell her that he saw a most gorgeous and beautiful woman on his way to work and then consider it his right to get angry if his wife is upset that he made the remark. A woman, on the other hand, would be considered loose and an immoral "whore" if she told her husband that she saw a most handsome man while on her way to work and could risk her whole marriage for making such a remark. The latest "honor" killing is nothing new. While there are no available statistics on the number of women killed because of family honor, these killings do take place.

Last month in Gaza, two young women were killed by their families on suspicion that they dishonored their families but it was only after the autopsy showed that the two were still virgins that their male relatives who killed them were arrested. Perhaps what is most disturbing in all this is the reaction of the women at the wake to these "honor" killings. While some admit knowing of male relatives who have extra-marital relations, they don't regard these relations as bringing dishonor to the family.

"Men are different," they tell me. "A woman, on the other hand, has nothing if she does not have honor." Somehow in their mind-set, their upbringing and their beliefs, these women don't regard themselves as on an equal footing with men. Sadly none of these women is educated. Most were married as teenagers, spending their lives being mothers and housewives. Most have teenage daughters who left school and are now married with children. They have raised their daughters to cook and clean and obey their husbands. "A woman without her husband is worthless," they insist.

What about educating their daughters and letting them work so they can be economically independent and have some experience in life? "With or without an education, they will end up housewives and mothers," they maintain. Often times, it is young women who pay the price of the years they spent cooped up at home and prevented from working and mingling with the opposite sex. It is these young women who have no life experiences who are most prone to making mistakes.

Hanan was 17 when she joined a popular committee in the Intifada and started attending mixed political meetings. A beautiful young woman who was always forced to stay home, Hanan was overwhelmed by the attention young men in her group suddenly paid her. One of these young men was a collaborator and he tried to start a relationship with Hanan in order to get her to work with him. She had the sense to refuse and when she did, he came to her house one night with three other men, all wearing masks, and beat Hanan and her sister. Hanan's family, who knew nothing about the situation, reacted by taking her out of school, even though she was in her last year in high school. From then on, they forbade her to leave the house. "My whole family treated me as if I were tainted even though I didn't do anything," complains Hanan. Her mother and many of her female relatives tried their best to get Hanan to marry any older widower or divorced man who came to propose. "They made me feel that I was worthless and that no man, if not divorced or a widower, would ever be interested in me. If the same thing had happened to one of my brothers, the family wouldn't have made him leave school and sit at home," she cried.

For four years, Hanan paid the price in silence. Her family treated her as a brainless, good-for-nothing idiot. Throughout this time, she was never able to speak frankly with her mother about how she felt. "You have shamed us," is all that her mother would say.

With the arrival of the Palestinian Authority, Hanan thought the end of her misery was near. Without the knowledge of her family, she went to the police station and spoke to one of the officers in charge. "My family thinks I was involved in collaboration but I wasn't. I want you to investigate and clear my name so I can start leading a normal life again," she told the officer. Promising to do his best, the officer told Hanan he needed to talk to her more at length and asked her to meet him at his house the following Friday. "Don't be afraid," he calmed her. "I live alone." Now suspicious of the officer's intentions, Hanan went to a friend, asking her what to do. Her friend advised her to never go near the officer again. "Your family would cut you to pieces if they found out you've been to see him," her friend told her. From the start, had Hanan felt she could go to her mother and tell her she was being harassed by a young man without the risk of turning her life into hell, events may have taken a different turn. Had Hanan been allowed to continue her schooling, her sense of worth would have improved. Had she been given the weapon of an education and the security of a job, she would have valued herself more. In the end, Hanan was lucky. A distant cousin, close to her age, married her nearly two years ago and she moved away with him. Hanan, of course, is a mother now. Will she educate her children? Will she teach her daughters that their worth as women is far greater than being married to a man? Will she teach them that women are not worthless without a man?

16   Celebrating Independence (1998)*

Whenever Palestinians celebrate any type of a national or religious event, it is hard to watch them and not feel an overwhelming surge of compassion. Old men on canes, elderly women with hearing aids, fashionably dressed schoolchildren, mothers with crying babies in their arms, and weary-looking men all turn out to watch. Their thirst for an occasion, any occasion that would ease their mundane daily routine is visibly unquenchable.

And so it was on November 15, the day marking the tenth anniversary of the Palestinian declaration of independence. With a clear sky, warm sun and no work or schools for the day, hundreds of Palestinians in the Bethlehem area converged on the parking lot of the Department of Transportation, across the street from Dheisheh Refugee Camp, to watch the 'independence' celebrations. Normally held at Bethlehem's Manger Square, the celebrations were moved to Dheisheh this year due to major construction at the Square.

From the early hours, the air was filled with a blend of sounds and sights. Schoolchildren were having a heyday with firecrackers; impossible to purchase under occupation but now sold to any child with the few shekels required to buy them. Young boys would wait for a group of giggling schoolgirls to walk by and then light a match to a firecracker and mischievously watch the girls jump in a feigned display of fear. Young children were roaming around freely, away from the watchful eyes of their parents. Whenever they saw a peddler selling corn-on-the-cob, Coca-Cola, or hot peanuts, they would suddenly go on a mad hunt for their parents amidst the crowds. Tugging at the skirts of their oblivious mothers, they would first ask for money, then cry and beg for it. Finally, after failing to get their mothers' attention, they would go into a fit, screaming at the top of their lungs in a desperate last attempt to get a shekel. Embarrassed by the sudden tantrums, the mothers would reluctantly relinquish some money but not before hissing into their children's ears, "Your father is going kill you when we get home."

* (First published in *Palestine Report*, November 20, 1998.)

Patriotic songs, memorized all too well by different generations of Palestinians, blurt from loudspeakers but do very little to deafen the noise from the crowds. Occasionally, the music is interrupted when someone in army fatigues grabs hold of the microphone to ask the crowd to clear the parking lot.

"The military parade is approaching, please move back," he repeatedly shouts. Nobody listens. The request is repeated yet again but still, nobody listens. "To all police and soldiers, please clear the crowd from the parking lot," the man finally yells in desperation. The police and soldiers oblige but cannot control the children who keep playing a cat-and-mouse game, running across the parking lot.

Finally, after much ado, the military parade arrives to the sound of drums and pipes. Some of the soldiers are brandishing guns with bayonets. The children suddenly fall silent and watch in awe. A young boy, dressed in military uniform, unexpectedly runs out of the crowd and joins one marching army unit. A policeman spots him and tries to move him away. The boy grabs the hand of the solider nearest to him, holds on tight, looks up at the policeman and dares him to remove him. The policeman smiles and walks away.

Suddenly, the news spreads. Several Palestinians, including Palestinian legislator Salah Tamari, suffered from tear-gas inhalation and two Israeli soldiers were injured during violent clashes with Israeli troops in the village of al-Khader, just a few meters down the street. The clashes erupted when Israeli soldiers fired tear gas at more than a hundred Palestinians attempting to block an Israeli bulldozer from uprooting a vineyard to build a new bypass road in an area scheduled for transfer to Palestinian rule under the Wye River Agreement. More than 4,000 dunums of Palestinian land are expected to be confiscated in the villages of al-Khader, Artas and Wadi Rahal to make way for By-pass Road 55 which, upon completion, would connect Israeli settlements in the area without going through Palestinian-controlled territory.

The local TV camera crews covering the celebrations race to al-Khader. A car brings Palestinian legislator Tamari to the UNRWA-operated health clinic in Dheisheh. From there, he is transferred to a local hospital. Other Palestinians suffering from tear-gas inhalation go to the hospital for treatment as well.

Khaled Azza, President of the Public Committee for the Defense of Land, appeals to the crowds to head for al-Khader. "We appeal to your conscience to head to al-Khader and stop the Israeli bulldozers," he shouts. About twenty men from Dheisheh, and only two of the three Palestinian legislators who had been at the 'independence' celebrations all morning, heed his call.

Some time later, the local TV crews are back. They walk around and interview people. "What is your impression of the celebrations?" they ask. People's answers vary. Some say they are good, others talk about the prisoners, while others talk about liberating the rest of Palestinian land. The fiery speeches, calling for the release of Palestinians from Israeli prisons, the end of settlement expansion and the right of the Palestinians to Jerusalem, continue but no one pays attention.

By early evening, the crowds still fill the parking lot. Different folklore dance troupes from various area villages entertain the crowds. The nearby bakery and restaurant report excellent business for the day. Parents send their sons to search for their sisters and bring them home because it is dark and girls should not go out at night unescorted.

By night, all is quiet. The music stops. The crowds go home and many adults suffer bad headaches from the daylong noise. Children go to bed happy. They all had a fabulous time and spent as much money as they do during the holy feasts of al-Fitr and al-Adha. Everyone turns on their TV to one of the local stations. If they're lucky, they'll watch themselves on the tube. Suddenly, someone realizes that the familiar faces of local leaders from the various political factions were nowhere to be seen. Someone else realizes that women and children under the age of 16 made up the majority of the crowd. Still, nobody cares.

Two young men walk home through Dheisheh's dark alleyways. "Do you remember how we used to celebrate the declaration of independence under occupation?" asks Kamal.

"Of course," recalls Khaled. "We would buy long rolls of scouring pads and use them as substitute flares. Do you remember how we would grab the edge of the scouring pad, swing it in the air and watch the little stars of light brighten the darkness of the night?"

"Man! The Israeli soldiers would go into a fit and come chasing after us," smiles Kamal.

Yeah," Khaled nods. "That was what real independence felt like, wasn't it?"

17   From Dheisheh to Jerusalem (1998)*

Sheikha finds a spot in the shade and sits down to catch her breath. The relatively short trip from Jerusalem to Dheisheh under the scorching July sun has sapped her aging, sick body. Without speaking, she motions her longtime friend Halimeh to sit next to her. Halimeh slumps down on the dusty rock. "We're almost home," she gasps. Sheikha doesn't answer. Her large bosom heaves and she winces from the pain. She closes her eyes and fantasizes about an ice-cold glass of water cooling her throat and her insides. She opens her eyes and licks her dry lips with her parched tongue. "Oh God Almighty! Have mercy on us from this awful heat," she whispers and grabs the edge of her white headcover to wipe her sweaty face.

The two women sit there, afraid to get up and face the sun that has been glaring at them all day. It wasn't so bad in the early hours of the morning when they started off for al-Aqsa Mosque in Jerusalem to attend the Friday prayer. But now, at 3 p.m., the heat was too much to bear and the thought of having to walk up the hill before reaching home was hellish. Nearly ten minutes pass before Sheikha shifts her weary body. She reaches down for the plastic shopping bag resting by her swollen feet. Four loaves of sesame bread stick out of the bag, looking dried and twisted. "Let's go," she tells Halimeh as she gets to her feet. The two women plod into the camp, as if pilgrims back from hard travels. "I'll see you next Friday," murmurs Halimeh as she and Sheikha part ways. "God willing! If we are alive," answers Sheikha as she bids her friend farewell.

Sheikha can hardly remember when the Israelis started imposing a siege on Jerusalem, making it impossible for West Bank Palestinians to get to the city without having to carry Israeli-issued permits and go through military checkpoints. But she vividly recalls when Jerusalem was simply there, accessible, reachable, and open to all Palestinians. "Even at the height of the Intifada, we didn't need permits," she says. "Can you imagine that? We used to come and go

* (First published in the *Jerusalem Quarterly File*, fall 1998.)

to Jerusalem as we pleased. Things were different then. Starkly different."

Between 1977 and 1989, Sheikha worked as a cleaning woman at Hebrew University. She and nearly ten other women from Dheisheh camp worked on the Mount Scopus campus, making the trip to Jerusalem six days a week for twelve straight years. "There were no checkpoints at the entrance to Jerusalem and no one ever stopped us to ask for permits," she recalls.

While no figures are available as to the number of Dheisheh refugees who used to work in Jerusalem in the 1970s, the number is believed to be much higher than it is today. Many Dheisheh nurses, UNRWA employees, journalists, construction and restaurant workers, and fruit pickers used to work in the city. Dheisheh refugees employed by UNRWA used to either work at UNRWA headquarters in Jerusalem or drive into Jerusalem to attend staff meetings. "Now we hold our meetings in Ramallah because the majority of UNRWA employees don't have permits to enter the city," says Hussein Shaheen, UNRWA's Camp Director in Dheisheh. Shaheen worked at UNRWA headquarters between 1973 and 1992 and used to drive his own car to work. Since 1992, Shaheen has been issued a three-month entry to Jerusalem only three times, but never a permit for his car.

"It is very difficult to get an entry permit for a human being, so imagine what it's like getting a car permit," he says.

Like most Dheisheh refugees, Shaheen hasn't been to Jerusalem in four or five years. "Jerusalem wasn't simply a place of employment, but a place where we went to attend conferences, workshops, book fairs, theater plays, and much more."

Rab'aa Manna', who worked with Sheikha at Hebrew University, also remembers.

"Jerusalem to us was the city next door. It was where we worked, where we went to pray on Fridays, and where we occasionally went shopping in the market of the Old City. Now, it feels like a far-away place, and America appears to be more accessible to us than Jerusalem is."

For several years now, Rab'aa has been going to Jerusalem only during the Month of Ramadan, and even then, she only goes on Fridays.

"I go to pray at al-Aqsa. I stay all day and attend three prayers." Rab'aa doesn't like making the trip. "Sometimes the Israeli soldiers at the Bethlehem checkpoint send us back, and we have to make a long detour on foot. I'm too old for this nonsense. I remember one time that we had to go down a valley and walk up a treacherous hill just to escape the soldiers who were in pursuit. I was sick for three days after that." Rab'aa hates the whole idea of permits and refuses to apply for one. "I'm in my late forties and a grandmother to 14 children. How can I possibly be a security threat to the Israelis if I go pray in Jerusalem?" she asks defiantly. "I always take my chances. If they let me through, then so be it, if not, then I sneak in." She laughs at the idea. "A woman like me has to sneak in! It sounds criminal, doesn't it?"

If sneaking in to pray at al-Aqsa is a crime, then the majority of the older women in Dheisheh are criminals. All the Palestinian grandmothers and great grandmothers in Dheisheh and elsewhere in Palestine are, in the eyes of the Israeli authorities, a threat to Israel's national security. If they were to take Israeli regulations seriously, they would all have to endure the nuisance of submitting applications for entry permits to Jerusalem and then be at the mercy of some Israeli officer who may, or may not, grant them a one-day entry permit into the city. There are no known cases where a Palestinian was issued a permit for the specific purpose of going to pray in Jerusalem. In Dheisheh, and throughout the West Bank, the increasing closure of Jerusalem since the Madrid talks in 1991 has had a profound impact on the Palestinian psyche and the way of life. Even at the height of the Intifada, Palestinians could get on the bus and ride into Jerusalem. "There would be severe clashes inside the camp, and we would go to Jerusalem without anyone asking us where we were going," recalls Sheikha. "Now, Jerusalem seems like a far-away city in some foreign land."

It is obvious to all Palestinians now that since the peace talks were initially launched, Israel has been pursuing a policy of isolating Jerusalem from the hearts and minds of West Bank and Gaza Palestinians. At first it was not entirely clear that it would be a sustained and systematic policy. At the start, when the Israelis began requiring permits from Palestinians to get into the city, many thought the closures were temporary. Soon, however, the systematic nature of the policy emerged. The Israelis made it next to impossible for students to obtain entry permits that would allow them to study at Jerusalem schools, colleges and universities. They also made it difficult for Palestinian buses and taxis to get permits, thus creating a situation where transportation into Jerusalem wasn't as easy as it used to be.

In addition, the Israelis made it increasingly difficult for medical patients to get permits to enter Jerusalem for medical treatment at al-Maqassed Hospital or any other Palestinian hospital in East Jerusalem. Palestinian refugees, for instance, used to get free referrals from UNRWA-operated clinics in the various camps for treatment at the Augusta Victoria Hospital on the Mount of Olives. But now, that too has changed. Because repeated closures have made it difficult for Palestinians to enter Jerusalem, UNRWA has started referring refugee patients to other hospitals in the West Bank. Bethlehem area refugees, for instance, are now referred to al-Ahli Hospital in Hebron and, in delivery cases, to the French Hospital in Bethlehem. Only when a particular treatment is not available in the West Bank are patients still referred to the Augusta Victoria, which has since been privatized. Furthermore, young women from the Bethlehem area, a 20-minute drive to downtown East Jerusalem, used to go shopping in Jerusalem, but now they go shopping in Bethlehem. Students at universities in Jerusalem have to sneak in to attend classes. In manifold and accumulating ways, the Israelis are obstructing and suffocating the everyday ways of life that have historically tied Palestinians to the city.

When you ask Dheisheh camp residents how long it has been since they've been to Jerusalem, the answers vary. Some say it has been four years, others say it has been five. "We can pack a bag and cross the Allenby Bridge into Jordan right now without even thinking about it, but we cannot even dream of hopping into a taxi and driving into Jerusalem," says Hiyam, a Dheisheh woman in her thirties who used to go into Jerusalem at least once a week to buy clothes at bargain prices from the Old City. "What is even more ridiculous is when relatives from Jordan or the Gulf States come to visit us. They have tourist visas and go to Jerusalem any time they like, but we cannot go with them," complains Hiyam. "They end up going sight-seeing on their own, and we sit at home and wait for them to come back and tell us what it felt like to spend a day in Jerusalem. It is the most absurd and insane situation I can think of." Hiyam's sister, Amal, works as a nurse at al-Makassed Hospital. "I rely on Amal to buy me anything I need from Jerusalem," explains Hiyam. "Sometimes she finds clothes at bargain prices. I try them on and if they don't fit, she takes them back and exchanges them. You'd think she's off to someplace in Europe and I'm asking her to buy me something that I can't get here."

Only a small number of construction workers and nurses, like Amal, work in Jerusalem and are issued permits. Others sneak past the military checkpoints in order to work inside the city. Each day they take a chance and risk getting caught. Sometimes they're lucky, other times they aren't. Sometimes the punishment is a night in prison, or a fine, or a good beating, or a few hours of punishment spent standing under the hot sun without a drink of water. It all depends on the mood of the Israeli soldier who catches the unlucky man. Meanwhile, it is Friday again. Dheisheh sleeps in on this relaxed one-day weekend and the alleys and streets rest from the snarl of traffic and the screams of children. The only people out and about this early in the morning are the grandmothers and great grandmothers. They walk down the hill in pairs or in groups of three or four. Their pace is slow but determined. Small, overstuffed shopping bags swing in their hands. A small pot of coffee, a bottle of iced water, home-baked bread, a few tomatoes, olives, and perhaps a piece of goat cheese: the nourishment they will have when they sit under the shade of the olive trees in the spacious courtyard of al-Aqsa Mosque in Jerusalem. First they'll attend the Friday sermon, pray, and then have their little picnic.

"My grandchildren asked for sesame bread, remind me to get some," Sheikha tells Halimeh as they emerge from Damascus Gate in the Old City of Jerusalem.

"My grandchildren want some too," Halimeh replies. "I don't know why their father can't get it for them from Bethlehem. They can eat it before it's dry."

"What a silly thing to say! They know they can get it from Bethlehem, but it won't be the same. The sesame bread we're bringing has the taste and aroma of Jerusalem. Don't you get it? That's what they want ..."

18   Making it in a Man's World (1998)

When Maha found out that her husband of six years was collaborating with the Israelis, she was devastated. Her immediate reaction was to ask for a divorce. But her mother, to the horror of the rest of the family, wouldn't let her.

"I'd rather my daughter be married to a collaborator than be divorced," was the mother's lame excuse.

So Maha found herself back with her husband and soon she was pregnant with her second child. The marriage did not last. Her husband was not only physically abusive of her but he was apparently still an unrepentant collaborator. When the Palestinian Authority arrested him on suspicion of collaboration, Maha packed her clothes and moved in with her family. This time around, she insisted on the divorce.

From the money she had saved from her good-paying job at a hospital in Jerusalem, Maha built a small, two-room apartment in her family's spacious garden. The alternative of renting an apartment elsewhere was, of course, out of the question and socially unacceptable. Divorced women in Palestine simply cannot live alone and expose themselves to all sorts of gossip.

Having settled down in her new place, Maha began her fight for a divorce. Her husband's family insisted on waiting until he came out of jail and when he did, more than a year later, Maha asked him for a divorce. He refused and for months on end, he would take Maha's children to stay with him, keeping them for a month at a time. Maha became irritable, nervous and she began to lose weight. She wanted a divorce and custody of her children. In April 1998, nearly two years after she moved into her new apartment, she got both. The price she had to pay was to give up her alimony and child support. She didn't care. She wanted to be free of the man, no matter what the cost.

With a full-time job of working and raising her children, Maha has gone back to university to finish her degree and is quite happy with her new life. She is also very happy to be financially independent of her family.

"If I hadn't had a job it would have been the end of me," she says. "I would have had to be at the mercy of my family, waiting for them to feed and clothe me."

Though Maha is a very strong-willed and independent woman, she is beginning to feel the effects of being a divorced woman in Palestine.

"I feel like I'm under constant scrutiny. I can't go out alone in the evenings unless it is with my parents or brothers," she explains. "It is as if people watch me to see if I make a mistake so they can criticize me."

In her late twenties, Maha does not think about the prospects of getting married again.

"Who wants to marry a divorced woman with two children?" she asks.

Indeed, most Palestinian women who are divorced don't get many marriage offers. If they do, it is either from an old widower or a divorced man who wants someone to take care of him and his children.

"Being a divorced woman is socially unacceptable," says Salwa who was divorced nearly ten years ago and has one son. "If I didn't have a job, my life would have been completely different," she says.

Indeed, it is their jobs that give these divorced women the financial independence they need. "My life would be terrible if I had to depend on my brothers for money. They would completely control me."

Like Maha, Salwa feels the social restrictions of being a divorced woman.

"I cannot go out in the evening to visit friends. If I do, people would be suspicious," she explains. "If I put on too much make-up, they'll wonder who am I putting it on for? The difficulties are immense."

A similar problem exists for Palestinian women who have reached their thirties and forties without getting married. Hala, 49, never got married and neither did two of her three sisters. The "girls", as people call them, live with their mother and all three work. But Hala is not happy with her life at home.

"Our house is always full of people and I never seem to have any privacy after a long day at work. My nephews and nieces come over and we are always running around cleaning after them," she says.

Hala would love to live alone. She has many girlfriends and likes to have them over but feels she cannot.

"If they come to visit me, they have to visit with my entire family." But living alone is out of the question, even for a woman Hala's age. "My relatives would be horrified if I rented a place on my own and immediately they would doubt my motives," she says. "If you are not married, then you have to be careful about every move you make. If you speak with a man, you have to look over your shoulder. If you laugh at a joke a man tells you, you have to make sure you don't laugh too loud. It is disgusting."

Although Hala has a full social calendar, her sisters don't.

"Majd and Riham go from the house to the office and back. They don't go out for meals, not even with their girlfriends," explains Hala.

Theirs is a dull and boring existence and I cannot imagine what they'll be like thirty years from now."

Today, Hala's sisters, both in their late thirties, still get occasional marriage offers. One time it is from a 60-year-old widower who needs a "maid" to look after him or, a man with two wives, a herd of children, and a desire to peeve both wives by marrying a third. This angers Hala.

"My sisters have many skills from cooking, to embroidering, to gardening, you name it. Yet a single man who is about their age never proposes. Everyone is looking for younger women in their late teens or early twenties and if my sisters do marry, it will be so that they can be slaves to a man who is basically looking for an old servant."

For these women, the future is unclear. They all work but none has any savings. They don't know what will happen to them when they reach an age when they can no longer earn a living.

"Who will take care of us?" they ask. No one has the answer.

19   Diving with a Splash (1998)[*]

It's that time of year again. The blazing hot sun and high tempera-
tures of 35 degrees Celsius, in the shade, are promising a long
sweltering summer. The story is all too familiar for the Palestinians:
summer means lots of dust, a blinding bright sun, barely any refuge
in the shade, and the same old problem of severe water shortages.
Welcome to another summer in the Palestinian Territories!

To keep cool during those long sizzling days, when one has to
think ten times before wasting precious water on a cold daily shower,
I switch on the TV to an Israeli channel and impatiently wait for the
commercial break. It finally arrives: a Coca-Cola commercial
showing attractive, tanned and slim Israelis at the beach, sun
bathing and splashing each other with a water hose. The deep blue
Mediterranean water shimmers in the background, so enticing, and
ever so inviting to a scorched Palestinian like me. The commercial
lasts for 30 seconds and that's all the time I need not only to feel
cool and refreshed, but also outraged. There is obviously no water
shortage in the Holy Land; you just have to be on the other side of
the Green Line to enjoy it.

I angrily turn off the TV, close my eyes, and pretend I'm surfing
the waves. Fantasy is the only sane escape from a sordid reality.
Suddenly the phone rings and rudely brings me back to the heat. It's
a friend who lives three blocks up the hill and she's asking if we have
any water. I tell her that the water has been cut off for three days.

"The water pressure was too low to reach the water reservoirs on
our rooftop without using an electric water pump," I explain.

"Well, the water never reached us and none of the private water
trucks I've called are willing to drive inside the refugee camp to sell
us water," Hourieh complains. "They say our streets are too narrow
and they're not willing to make the trip unless I pay them [U.S.] $52."

This price is nearly triple the actual cost of the water but the
private water providers know that people will pay because they must
drink. They also make you pay for more water than you can store. If,
for instance, you only have five water reservoirs on your rooftop,

* (First published in *Palestine Report*, May 28, 1998.)

they'll bring you enough water for ten reservoirs, charge you for it and then drive away with the extra to sell it elsewhere. God forbid you suggest sharing the water with the neighbor!

So why don't our local authorities do something about this outrageous exploitation?

Well, they are doing something. Last summer, several local officials implored the public through the local press to file complaints against these money-mongers; but no legal, or any other, action has been taken to stop this annual exploitation of an already exhausted public. By the end of this summer, the same officials are likely to implore the public again. By doing so, they're sure to catch two birds with one stone: get their names in the papers, and appear to be taking action on an issue that concerns all segments of our society.

Meanwhile, my friend Hourieh paid the $52 for her water and purchased an additional five water reservoirs for $137 so as not to lose any of the water that she will now be forced to purchase till next winter. "I don't know whether to be more depressed because I have an endless pile of laundry to wash or to be depressed because $189 out of my husband's $500 monthly salary is already gone in a blink."

As it turned out, Hourieh complained all too soon. Ten days later, the water reservoirs on her roof were empty again. But she didn't really care because she had placed three of her new water reservoirs in the garden and could haul water in a bucket to do her housework.

"This is silly," retorted her husband Nabieh when he got home from work. "Why should you haul water all day when we can pump the water to the reservoirs on the roof?"

Without wasting any time, Nabieh borrowed a water pump from a neighbor, a long hose from another and went to work.

"When I open the cover and place the hose inside, turn on the water," he shouted at his wife as he climbed nearly two meters to reach the top of the reservoir. But as soon as Nabieh spoke, he lost his balance and came crashing down on the concrete roof, breaking both his arms.

For three weeks now, and still another three weeks to go, Nabieh's arms will remain in a cast. He needs his wife's help to light a cigarette, drink water, eat and go to the toilet. But it is the darn heat that's killing him. Sitting around in 35-degree weather with the heavy weight of two casts is just too much to take. But he has to grin and bear it, especially that his house is always full of concerned friends and relatives who drop by to wish him a speedy recovery.

Dealing with the influx of visitors has drained Hourieh. She has had to cook meals for her guests, serve refreshments, clean house, take care of her three young kids, buy groceries, help Nabieh and then welcome everyone with a big smile.

But neither Nabieh nor Hourieh is smiling. In the first three weeks since his fall, they've spent nearly $750 on medical expenses, food and beverages, and they've had to purchase more water and hire someone to fix their water reservoirs. Why? Because when Nabieh lost his balance and fell, he accidentally broke the pipe that connects the water reservoirs together.

With nothing else to do, Nabieh sits in front of the TV all day and keeps switching channels. It is summertime in Israel too and commercials showing Israelis splashing around at the beach and in swimming pools pop up on the screen every few minutes.

"Take us swimming Daddy," blurts 5-year-old Alaa' who hasn't left Nabieh's side ever since he witnessed his nasty fall.

"Do you want to swim in a pool or in the sea?" asks Nabieh.

"Can you dive in the sea and do it with a splash?" wonders the boy.

"I don't know," smiles Nabieh. "I've never been swimming."

"That's O.K. Daddy, I'll take you when I'm a man."

20　Life's Four Seasons (1998)[*]

The argument becomes heated. "I was by Ali's hospital bed when he died and I'm entitled to the *nkisa*," Mustafa roars.

"I don't care where you were. I was the one who arrived at Ali's house first," bellows Hussein.

"Take it easy guys," Khaled intervenes. "There is no need to make a scene. Ali's father is on his way and he'll tell us who's getting the *nkisa*."

The hour was close to dawn as the men stood in the darkened alley, waiting for the verdict. Who is going to cook the meal of fresh meat and rice for Ali's family following his burial the next day? This old habit, known as *nkisa*, is one family's way of honoring another family when death takes a loved one. It is an honor for which families vigorously compete; once taken, the *nkisa* remains in the deceased family's debt until they can repay it when someone from the other family dies.

The cries and wails of the women at Ali's house pierce the night silence. A car approaches and comes to a stop.

"May God rest his soul," the men tell Ali's father as he steps down from the car.

After shaking hands with each of the men, the old man speaks.

"My friends, I know that none of you falls short of doing his honorable duty, but in all fairness I have to tell you that Mustafa is the one entitled to take the *nkisa*. All of you know that, according to our customs, the man who is present at the moment of death is the one who gets it."

Hussein starts to argue, but the other men silence him. The matter is settled. For the next three days and nights, Ali's house is packed with an endless line of mourners who've come to pay their respects. The women sit together and offer Ali's wife, daughters, sisters, and daughters-in-law their sympathy and comfort. The men gather in another room while Ali's sons and male relatives serve coffee and put away the sacks of rice and sugar that were brought. The constant presence of people seems to absorb the family's initial shock over

[*] (First published in *The Link* by Americans for Middle East Understanding, May–June 1999.)

their loss. Mourning the dead is not a private matter, but one that is shared by the extended family, neighbors, and friends. Less than two weeks after Ali's death, many of the women who went to console his wife go to visit Um Issa, carrying gifts. Her daughter-in-law has just given birth to a baby boy and the women join her in the celebration of this new life.

At the beginning, I had a tough time understanding how the people of Dheisheh could cry with someone one day and then celebrate with someone else the next. But ever so slowly, I began to realize that Dheisheh's small world personifies the meaning of life and death. Death, like winter, makes the tree branches go bare. Then comes spring, or birth, bringing with it new blooms into the world. This is life. People accept it as such and their attitude toward this change of seasons is so very touching and endearing. Maybe it is the fact that everyone has been living together on this small 90-acre stretch of land these past 51 years that makes death so bearable. Ahmed, my husband, was born and raised in the same house we live in today. His neighbors have been the same neighbors all these years. Throughout this time, the children grew up, married, had children of their own, grandparents passed away, and parents themselves became grandparents. While you feel pain in seeing someone you love leave this world, you also watch his children grow and become men. It is a view of the cycle of life at its best. It is simple, yet forever forceful and continuously present for all of us to observe.

Perhaps it is this sense of safety that makes Dheisheh feel like home to a stranger like me. I moved between 3 countries and 17 houses and apartments in my 39 years of life. I don't know the fate of my high-school friends in Amman and I lost contact with many of my college friends in the United States. There simply has been no continuity and, therefore, no sense of belonging or safety in my life.

The opposite is true for Ahmed. His friends back in the first grade are still his friends today. They played hide-and-seek together, resisted the occupation together, and went to prison together. Today, they are building professional careers together and even doing their graduate studies together.

"How can you stand living in a run-down place like Dheisheh after living in Washington?" is a question I'm constantly being asked by Americans and Europeans who visit me in the camp.

The answer is simple really: whenever I ride the bus back from Bethlehem after going to town to run some errands, I'm always confronted with the same feeling. The moment the bus stops at

Dheisheh and I get off, I feel a sense of relief. The moment I cross the street and walk inside the camp, I feel like the whole place is my home. I can walk here blindfolded and not worry about falling; I can leave my house unlocked and not worry about getting robbed because there is no crime here; I can turn the corner to my house and be certain that the kids next door will come running to me with their warm greetings.

During dark moments when I'm melancholy or burdened with the responsibilities of life, a child's knock on the front gate saves me from myself.

"Who is it?" I ask, even though I know who my young visitor is.

"It is I, Zuzu," comes the sweet voice of the 4-year-old boy from next door.

"What do you want?" I tease.

"Open up. I got you the newspaper from the store."

Zuzu marches into the house, hands me the newspaper and walks right into the kitchen.

"Where are the bananas?" he asks.

"We're out," I smile.

"So how about boiling me an egg?" he says shyly.

"The best egg for the best Zuzu," I say, as I kneel down and give him a bear hug.

Wrapping his small arms around my neck and planting wet kisses on my cheeks, Zuzu sighs, "Oh, Aunt Muna, you're my darling."

I don't know why, but I cry each time.

21   Checkpoint Jerusalem (1999)[*]

My last trip to Jerusalem was in March 1995. I remember the day quite well. It was unseasonably warm, and I was scheduled to meet a British film producer at her rented flat near the Old City. Annie and I were finishing up work on the subtitles for a television documentary film about the Palestinian–Israeli conflict for Channel Four TV in London.[1] After spending several hours putting the final touches to our work, we went up on the roof of the two-storey house to eat a late, cold lunch. Annie was flying back to London the next day, and after relaxing in the late afternoon sun, I kissed her goodbye and walked down to the main street to catch the bus that would drop me off near my house in Dheisheh Refugee Camp just outside Bethlehem. Little did I know that glorious March afternoon that I was riding out of Jerusalem for the last time!

Don't get me wrong. It isn't that I've moved away to another country. On the contrary, I still live in Dheisheh, and Jerusalem, the city where I was born, is still an insanely close 15-minute drive to the north. So what has prevented me from going back to the city where I was born? The reason is rather simple really. Like countless other Palestinians, I lack the proper documents, entry permit, call it whatever you like, to present to the Israeli soldiers stationed around the clock at the military checkpoint that separates Bethlehem from Jerusalem. Now a permanent fixture, the checkpoint was erected back in 1991 to tighten Israel's control over Jerusalem and to control the flow of Palestinians into the Holy City. No Palestinians residing outside the municipal border imposed by Israel in 1967 are allowed entry without a special permit issued by the Israeli military authorities for periods extending from several hours to three months.

Now anyone who lives on the West Bank or has visited the place knows that Israeli military checkpoints certainly do not stop Palestinians from getting to Jerusalem if they are keen on getting there. Sneaking past checkpoints is commonplace, and I, for one, have

* (Segments of this chapter were first published in the *Jerusalem Quarterly File*, summer 1999, in an article titled "Checkpoint Jerusalem".)
[1] *Holy Lands* is a trilogy produced by October Films in London in 1995. It includes three episodes: Troubled Peace, Children of Abraham and Victims of Peace.

always envied my friends who deliberately disregard the soldiers and their ready-to-fire guns and walk on often long and windy dirt paths just to get to their destination. It seems to be a Palestinian trait, one that I have come to greatly admire, to break Israeli occupation laws. If an ordinary Palestinian wants to go to Jerusalem to shop, pray, visit a doctor, or work, no lack of permit or presence of a checkpoint will stand in his or her way. Such are the subtle ways of resisting a mean-spirited occupation.

But this method of entry does remain "illegal" and, at best, could mean being forced to turn back to the West Bank if caught and, at worst, could lead to the arrest and detention of the person who attempts it. More importantly, why should the Palestinians have to "sneak" into the Holy City? Shouldn't peace with Israel mean that they can enter the Holy City as freely as Israelis enter the Palestinian Territories? So much for "peace" changing our lives!

I remember back in the first Intifada of 1987 when it was habitual for us in Dheisheh to spend many long days, and sometimes weeks, under constant Israeli military curfew. Our houses in Dheisheh are clustered close to one another, making it easy for people to speak to one another through windows, rooftops and small, open courtyards. This, of course, allows for little privacy, and we used to always joke about how the close proximity of the houses to each other means that your neighbors can hear you when you snore or sneeze.

During the treacherously long days of curfew, our next-door neighbor, Abed, would stand in his entryway and shout over to my husband, Ahmed, as he sat drinking coffee under the grapevine in our open courtyard.

"Do you want go for a walk in Bethlehem?" Abed would shout.

"Is the coast clear?" Ahmed would shout back.

After making sure that no Israeli army patrol was in sight, the two would sneak out and head for Bethlehem for no apparent reason other than wanting to stretch their legs. Every time they took off, I was wrought with fear for Ahmed's safety. Being caught by an Israeli army patrol for breaking the curfew was no joke and usually resulted in a severe and solid beating, arrest, and even detention. One day I had had enough and tried to stop Ahmed from going.

"It is stupid of you to go out when you don't have a good reason to!" I cried.

"Even if we want to go and have ourselves an ice-cream cone, then that's a good enough reason. When will you understand that the occupation will never stop us from living our lives?" Ahmed angrily yelled back.

I envied him his courage and wished that I could be so bold and daring. But I wasn't. For me, the idea of breaking a curfew or sneaking into Jerusalem without a permit literally fills me with an uncontrollable physical fear. It could be because I did not grow up under occupation and just wasn't used to it. It also could be that after living in the United States for twelve years, I was accustomed to being a citizen with civil rights and a 911 phone number that I could dial so the police could come to my rescue if I was ever in any physical danger. Whatever the reason, I've never gotten accustomed to the sight of the Israeli soldiers, with their loaded guns. Somehow the notion of facing a might-be trigger-happy soldier has always made my legs go numb, my hands shake and my stomach twist in knots. I don't think I have ever known any fear like it.

Adding to my existing fear was the fact that I was not considered a legal resident of the West Bank and I was constantly afraid of being caught by the soldiers and deported back to the United States. Although I was born in Jerusalem in 1959 to Palestinian parents, who were also born in the country, I am one of hundreds of thousands of Palestinians who were outside the West Bank and the Gaza Strip when it fell under Israeli occupation in June 1967. In order to prevent Palestinians, even those who happened to be away on a brief business trip, from returning to the West Bank and Gaza to be counted in the census, the Israelis opted instead to consider us as Palestinians in "absentia", forcing us to become refugees for the second time in 19 years. And what this means, of course, is that we are not considered residents and cannot, therefore, hold West Bank or Gaza identification cards.

Ironically, and like so many other ironies about our predicament, it is being a citizen of the United States that allows me to be here in the West Bank and not because it is my birthright as a Palestinian. But even as an American of Palestinian origin, it is not easy to obtain legal residency in the West Bank. The Israelis are not known to give annual residency status to, let's say, foreigners who are married to local Palestinians. Consequently, thousands of Palestinian-Americans, and other Palestinians with foreign passports, are forced to leave the country every three months and re-enter on a new, three-month tourist visa in order to maintain their legal status. This method is both quite costly and impractical for anyone who lives here for an extended period of time. One alternative is to apply for family reunification through one's husband or an immediate family member who holds a West Bank identification card. But family reunification applications are left to the Israeli authorities to approve or reject and even in the rare occasions when they are approved, the decision could take the Israelis years to make, thus reinforcing the separation of wives from husbands, and children from parents.

The idea that it is up to the Israelis to decide whether or not I'll be allowed to reside in my country of birth was always unacceptable to me and between 1990 and 1993, I remained in the West Bank without a valid tourist visa. Then one day in mid-1993, when I was heading to my office at *al-Fajr* English weekly in East Jerusalem, an Israeli officer at the Bethlehem checkpoint noticed that my American passport carried an expired visa. He refused to let me into Jerusalem and I had no choice then but to report to the Israeli military administration in Bethlehem.

"Who do you think you are to stay here all this time without a visa?" asked the officer in charge.

"I'm a Palestinian settler," I replied. "I have a right to live here."

The officer, clearly displeased, didn't say anything. He simply asked me to pay a fine for "over-extending" my "stay in Israel" and advised me to apply for family reunification.

"You're lucky that the Israeli Supreme Court has issued a decision whereby people like you who married West Bank Palestinians before August 1990 cannot be deported," he told me.

I never knew what happened to the family reunification application that I filed in the summer of 1994. For some strange reason, there is no computer record that the application was ever filed. But I really didn't care. In mid-December 1995, Israelis troops redeployed from Bethlehem as part of the Oslo Agreement and I was under the illusion that I would have my wings back and fly again.

While the West Bank was one large area known as such prior to Oslo, the agreement and subsequent troop redeployment divided each district in the West into three different zones. Major West Bank cities became known as Zone A (under complete Palestinian control); a few West Bank villages became known as Zone B (under Palestinian civil control and Israeli security control); and the remaining majority of the West Bank became known as Zone C (under complete Israeli control).

Suddenly, square concrete blocks with ugly yellow and brown markings became our guidelines for which roads in the district of Bethlehem are controlled by the Palestinian Authority and therefore safe to roam free in, and which streets are under Israeli control where no Palestinian wanted by the Israeli authorities for one reason or another, would dare venture into. And just as suddenly, I was not only afraid to venture into nearby Jerusalem, I became fearful of leaving the 160 square meters that make up Zone A in the district of Bethlehem.

How would I explain to a mean-spirited Israeli soldier why the visa stamp on my U.S. passport expired in early 1995? What would I do if the soldier decided to take me away? What would I do if the Israelis decided to deport me? I had vowed to never leave Palestine except of my own free will, and if becoming a prisoner inside 160 square meters was the price I had to pay then I was going to pay it. Anything was better than giving the Israelis the satisfaction of deciding for me whether or not I could continue to live in my own country.

And so here I am, a prisoner in my bantustan prison cell since December 1995. The only world I've been to these past four years is the small world of Dheisheh Refugee Camp and the city of Bethlehem, the town of Beit Jala and the town of Beit Sahour. Jerusalem, Gaza, Israel and the rest of the world have all been off-limits to me all this time.

For a journalist accustomed to making trips to Jerusalem, Ramallah, Nablus, Hebron, and Gaza in search of a story, my immobility served a fatal blow to my work. No longer able to work for newspapers in Jerusalem or work as a researcher for foreign TV networks, I found myself sitting at home with nothing to do. Between March 1995 and July 1997, my life centered on washing the dishes, going shopping and drinking morning coffee with my neighbors. I felt like a worthless sap and ever so slowly, I felt that my brain was rotting like a stale vegetable. I was always a career woman, and I wasn't accustomed to merely being a housewife. Since I had no children, I was also unable to feel that my life had any worth, at least as a mother.

Naturally, I began descending into depression. I wanted a way out, a way back into my profession as a journalist that I loved so much. But I didn't know how I could work when I couldn't go anywhere.

By the summer of 1997, I was suffering from such low self-esteem that I knew I either had to fight back or dig myself a deep, black hole, crawl under it and die. As at so many other times in my life, destiny stepped in and rescued my wretched soul at the very last moment when it was just about to break. A friend helped me reach an agreement with *Palestine Report*, an English weekly published in East Jerusalem, to send them weekly articles from Bethlehem. I was thrilled to have a job that didn't require venturing outside Bethlehem. Two months later, I sold my antiquated computer and bought a new one, equipped with a modem. Through email and the Internet, I was able to completely turn my life around. Now my articles appear regularly in *Palestine Report* and *Middle East International* in London as well as in other publications in Paris, Jerusalem and London. True, I am an immobile journalist, but a journalist nonetheless.

Although I am still a prisoner in my bantustan prison cell and occasionally want to scream from the frustration of not being able to get out and at least see a different scenery than the one I've been seeing these past four years, I feel very triumphant and extremely alive! I do all my interviews over the phone and by fax and I research my articles by using the magical world of the Internet. I now know that I don't need an Israeli permit to have a life. I also know that there always is a way to resist the occupation. It takes perseverance to find a light at the end of a tunnel and if you are Palestinian, it simply means that your tunnel is longer and your light is farther away than you thought; but it is there nevertheless. No occupation, no matter how cold and cruel, can make the light go away. It is part of human nature to seek it out and see it.

I suppose now I finally understand what Ahmed meant when he used to insist on breaking the Israeli military curfews, regardless of his reason. I now also understand why checkpoints don't prevent Palestinians from reaching Jerusalem. It is a survival mechanism. It is a part of human nature. Either you muster all your mental scruples and emotional strength to find a place for yourself under the sun, or you succumb to defeat. It is all either white or black. There are absolutely no shades of gray in between. Absolutely none.

A well-known Israeli peace activist came to visit me in Dheisheh last year at a time when the Palestinian Territories were completely sealed off following a suicide bombing in Jerusalem.

"Didn't the soldiers at the checkpoint warn you against entering our territory considering the tension in the air?" I asked.

"They tried, but I coaxed them into letting me in," he smiled triumphantly.

"Too bad we don't have a Palestinian checkpoint to turn you back," I remarked.

"What do you mean?" he asked, surprised.

"Well, how in the hell are you going to really feel what we have to go through if you don't go through it yourselves?" I lashed out. "If I were in charge at the Palestinian Authority, I would require all Israelis to obtain a special permit from the Palestinians before entering our areas."

My Israeli friend wasn't amused. "You must be joking?"

"No, I'm dead serious. Just as we need your permits, if we can get them, in order to come visit you in Tel Aviv, you should also be obliged get permits, from us, to come visit us in the West Bank. But Oslo doesn't even give the Palestinians the right to arrest you for a traffic violation when you are in the West Bank. All we are authorized to do is to turn you over to the Israeli police."

"Well, if you'd like to go to Jerusalem or Tel Aviv, I'll take you. The soldiers won't speak to you if you are with me," he offered.

"So you'll sneak me in like I'm some kind of a criminal. No thanks. I'll only go to Jerusalem and Tel Aviv when I can get in my car and drive there as a free woman, and not because an Israeli, any Israeli, will allow it to happen."

My Israeli friend of nearly 14 years has not been back to Dheisheh since. Frankly, I don't care. Often I feel as if even the best-intentioned Israelis are happy to have us stay in our small bantustan prison cells, and then to come show solidarity with us and issue press statements to the world demanding that we get our rights. For isn't it curious that there hasn't been a single mass Israeli demonstration at one of the numerous Israeli checkpoints leading from the West Bank to Jerusalem to demand freedom of travel for the Palestinians? If five thousand Israelis were to occasionally show up at a given checkpoint, instead of the handful who normally do, wouldn't they force the Israeli government to pay attention?

Instead, the Palestinians are the ones who are miraculously expected to forgo their sense of belonging to Jerusalem. "Out of sight, out of mind" is supposed to make us forget the cobblestoned roads of the Old City. Somehow, the distance is intended to obliterate from our nostrils the aromatic smell of spices in the ancient market. Absence is meant to fade the image of Jerusalem's old homes with their tilted redbrick roofs from our minds.

Somehow, we are to forget the landmark newspaper stand on the sidewalk across from Damascus Gate and the peddlers selling oven-broiled eggs and sesame bread. And quite magically, we are to lose the sense of awe that touches even the non-believers among us whenever the shimmering golden Dome of the Rock blinds our vision and fools us into thinking that it has taken the place of the sun.

Increasingly, as we head toward a final settlement deal that is unlikely to offer us a more dignified "peaceful" solution than what previous peace deals have offered us so far, we find ourselves forced to face a very hard fact. Israel is moving along with its "Greater Jerusalem" scheme, with the full blessing of the United States, in order to squeeze the city inside the ironclad fist of mushrooming settlements and make it physically impossible to negotiate in any final status deal.

And while we wait for the future to reveal to us the fate of our Holy City, we remain locked inside our bantustan prison cells, fooling ourselves into believing that we no longer belong to Jerusalem, while knowing in our hearts and minds that we will always belong.

Yes we do belong, damn it!

We belong just as our parents and grandparents belonged before us. Grandpa Attallah lived in Jerusalem all his life. My best childhood memories are those of the times spent with him. Our walks on Salah id-Din Street and stopover at Nasser id-Din Supermarket for chocolates and candy must have really left an impression since, quite unconsciously, I would stop to buy Cadbury and Mars bars there whenever I went to Jerusalem in the past. Also memorable were our visits to the Church of the Holy Sepulcher to light candles on lazy Sunday afternoons. How many times did I go back to light a candle for Grandpa? I haven't counted. Nor have I tried to count the endless times when I found myself walking up Nablus Road and stopping next to the American Consulate. There, across the street, stands the house where my mother lived as a child – now, of course, occupied by an Israeli family.

Without planning to, I look at the upstairs windows and try to guess which room was mother's. And then I can almost see her, a charming girl with a pretty dress swaying slowly on the swing. Or is she reading in the garden? As I try to make up my mind, two young children come darting out of the house. Their small talk in Hebrew confuses me. Where did Mom go?

I swallow hard and feel a twinge of pain from the knot in my throat. As I walk away, I glance back at the house, longing to be inside. "This is our Jerusalem," I whisper to myself, feeling intoxicated by my inability to really make it mine.

Oh dear God! When will sobriety come?

22 The Pope in Our Midst (2000)

Tuesday, March 21, 2000
Dheisheh gets ready for the Pope

Dear Diary,

I can't even begin to describe the atmosphere in Dheisheh as the camp prepares to receive Pope John Paul II tomorrow. It is so exciting to be here, considering that this is the first time in the history of the camp that a Holy See has visited Dheisheh.

A welcoming committee has been set up in the camp to prepare for the Pope's visit. With all the preparations underway, Dheisheh's public library was turned into a base of operations nearly ten days ago. But today, the place is a real beehive.

In one corner, a couple of young artists from the camp are painting, on large reinforced cardboard, house keys, tents and other symbolic depictions of the refugee experience. They will display their work all along the route that the Pope's procession is scheduled to take as he arrives in Dheisheh tomorrow. In another corner, a group of young people are leaning over poster-sized colored cardboard and writing the names of the more than 42 villages that Dheisheh's refugees were forced to flee in 1948; villages which were destroyed by Israel during and after the 1948 War. Young guys grab rolls of tape and a pile of posters showing the Pope and Palestinian President Arafat, and go off to hang them on the windows of shops, garage doors and wherever else they can make the tape stick.

Ziad sits at the computer and writes the program of events in Arabic. I then take over and translate the program into English. Mohammed makes tens of copies of the printed program to hand out to all the press coming to Dheisheh to report on the Pope's visit. Several people are acting as guides to the numerous journalists who are flooding the camp. Foreign journalists, TV cameramen and radio correspondents have been steadily coming to Dheisheh these past ten days.

The press interview every refugee they come across. "What do you think of the Pope's visit?" they ask. The responses convey a feeling of excitement for having someone as important as the Holy See in the camp, but also make it clear that the refugees don't think the Pope will openly speak up in favor of the refugees' right of return to their homeland. "He isn't going to do anything for us," they tell the journalists.

A group of young guys go out with spray cans to write graffiti on the walls around the camp. One guy writes: "Dheisheh, Jabalya, Sabra, Wihdat, Yarmouk are real evidence of half a century of inhumanity." Another writes: "Sorry Pope! We will not name any of our alleys after you. Camps can't last forever!"

Another group of artists are drawing murals on the concrete walls of the houses that the Pope will pass. My house is one of them. Sanitation workers, employed by the United Nations Relief & Works Agency, remove the garbage and debris from our street. The women in the neighborhood stand by their doorways and watch. They holler at the workers, "We wish we had an important visitor every day so you would clean our streets all the time." More women of different ages gather around and complain about the filth in the streets, the indifference of UNRWA to maintain cleanliness, and they curse under their breath.

Cartons with hundreds of white T-shirts that the committee had ordered finally arrive. A group of young guys bring them inside the public library and stack them in a corner. Mohammed starts opening the boxes and handing out T-shirts to a bunch of young kids who suddenly appeared out of thin air. Some T-shirts have a print of the Pope and Arafat, others have a print of the Pope by himself and others have the words "Right of Return" printed on the front in black.

Meanwhile, over at Dheisheh's two schools, the teachers and students are getting ready for the March of the Keys. The march will start off from the camp at noon and kids will carry the old keys to their family homes in '48-Palestine, as well as placards with the names of their villages. The march is intended to send a message to the world that the refugees will never give up their right of return.

The marchers, mostly school children, chant, "The right of return is sacred" as they walk through the camp's alleys. I join them and take pictures of the kids. As we approach the northern edge of the camp, we see a helicopter approach Arafat's helicopter pad, built just up the hill from the camp. The kids suddenly make a mad dash and run for the hill. "President Arafat is here," they scream euphorically. The press, myself included, run with them. We are all caught up in the excitement. Two Palestinian policemen shoo everyone away. The kids are getting dangerously close to the landing pad. But no one listens. The helicopter lands and it turns out that Arafat isn't on it. The pilot is simply practicing for tomorrow's big event. Disappointed, the kids suddenly lose interest in the march. Young girls holding single red roses in their hands decide to call it a day. It is Mother's Day today and they want to go home and give the roses to their mothers.

But they'll be back out on the streets in the evening. Stages will be erected on the main Jerusalem–Hebron road across from the camp and there will be nationalistic music and songs. Peddlers will be out there, selling corn-on-the-cob, Coca Cola and falafel sandwiches. The atmosphere in the camp feels like that of a national holiday.

Last night, Vatican and Palestinian security drove by our street. They were testing the Popemobile, I suppose to see if the expensive car can easily drive through the uneven and badly paved alleys.

For the past three to four days, our street has been packed with reporters, filming and taking pictures of the route that the Pope will take. I still can't believe that Pope John Paul II will pass right by my house.

After Israeli extremists vandalized a helicopter pad to be used by the Pope in Jerusalem, members of the Israeli press tried hard to get someone, anyone in the camp, to say something negative about the Pope's visit. They were terribly disappointed. The refugees were looking forward to it. True, they didn't have high expectations of the visit, but the fact that Dheisheh was singled out from all the refugee camps in the West Bank and Gaza to be visited by the Pope was a real honor.

In the past days, what has really been the most wonderful experience is the group effort that has gone into getting ready for the Pope. Camp residents, young and old, male and female, though not as many women as I would have liked to see, are all doing their thing, each in his or her area of expertise. It is heartwarming to watch the team effort being put into this. It makes my heart smile with pride.

*   *   *

Wednesday, March 22, 2000
The Big Day is Here

Dear Diary,

The big day is finally here. At 4 p.m. Pope John Paul II will be in our refugee camp. The hustle and bustle in this place is endless. Schools are out today and many people aren't planning to go to work, primarily because the roads will be closed in front of traffic. Security is very tight, but the atmosphere is of one big holiday.

Starting at 5:30 a.m. a police car has been driving through our alley asking residents to remove their cars. Until late last night, construction workers were laying stone tiles and stone steps around Dheisheh's Martyrs' Monument. The monument is located right next to the camp entrance that the Pope will drive through. All the dirt and debris near the monument has been removed. Neither UNRWA nor the Palestinian authority ever paid so much attention to Dheisheh. Keeping the camp clean for its residents simply isn't a priority for them. But now with the Pope's visit, they care, at least for the day.

Early yesterday, municipal workers from Bethlehem installed traffic lights at the entrance. The traffic lights don't work yet but maybe they will some day. At least they are installed. This was the highlight of the day for many camp residents. Several pedestrians, including children, were either killed or injured by speeding cars. Camp residents have been demanding the installation of traffic lights for years. If the Pope were to come visit every day, then we would have clean streets and traffic lights.

The murals on the walls are ready. Palestinian and Vatican flags are up. The invitations to the official reception at Dheisheh's Boys' School have been handed out – those without an invitation cannot enter the school where security is expected to be very tight.

Everything is perfect except for the weather, which suddenly turned from sunny and warm, to somewhat cold and drizzly. But come rain or shine, Dheisheh will be in the limelight today as millions of people around the world follow the Pope's visit to the camp. And although no one can predict what the Pope will say about the Palestinian refugee issue, the message of Dheisheh's refugees is already loud and clear: WE WILL NEVER GIVE UP OUR RIGHT OF RETURN.

It is the loudest and clearest message visible in this place.

*   *   *

Friday, March 24, 2000
Dheisheh, The Pope and the Clashes

Dear Diary,

This diary entry is one day late but I felt like a zombie yesterday following the events in Dheisheh on Wednesday, 22 March, 2000. Digesting the fact that the Pope was here amongst us, then witnessing the clashes between camp residents and police, took time to sink in.

Wow! What a day.

It started out perfectly. The atmosphere in the camp was so festive all day. Schools were out. Flags and posters were up. Television crews and journalists were all over the place. Men, women and children in the camp were out and about. We were waiting impatiently for the hour of the Pope's arrival, changed at the last minute from 4 p.m. to 5 p.m.

In the afternoon, members of the Palestinian police and various security forces took their positions at all the locations where the Pope was going to pass. A few days earlier, there was a rumor in the camp that all the rooftops along the street where the Pope was going to pass were going to be filled with police and security. This wasn't the case. The only people up on the rooftops were the residents, their relatives and friends. The number of police and security on our street wasn't as substantial as we anticipated. On the contrary, it was a very reasonable number and much less than what we expected. The crowds and most of the police and security were down on the main Jerusalem–Hebron road near the entrance leading to the street I live on, and near the school where the Pope was going to be officially received.

I went up on the rooftop with my friends Loren and Mary, an American couple. With our cameras ready, we waited to get a glimpse of the Pope. Suddenly someone shouted that the Pope was arriving. Next thing we knew the Popemobile, followed by a long line of very fancy VIP cars drove, for the first time ever, up our street.

I kept snapping pictures, and only took my eye away from the lens long enough to see the Pope's head right underneath me. I couldn't believe it! Pope John Paul II coming up the street that we walk on every day. Gee! What a feeling. We thought that Arafat would be visible to the crowds and wave to us, but we later found out, to our surprise, that Arafat didn't drive through the camp with the Pope. Instead, he arrived directly at the school.

As the Popemobile turned the corner up the hill, Loren, Mary and I made a mad dash for the school. We had tickets to get in. There was a bit of pushing and shoving at the gate, but it is at these moments that being a woman comes in handy. We kept trying to reach the gate until some guy shouted, "Make way for the women." We were inside.

I was surprised that the schoolyard wasn't as packed as I thought it would be. The Pope was already there. The number of issued tickets didn't exceed 400–500, and they were sent both to people from the camp and to guests from outside the camp.

We couldn't see the Pope from where we stood so we climbed on the school rooftop where all the journalists were. We had a perfect view of the Pope as he addressed the crowd. His speech, surprisingly not translated into Arabic, was hard to understand. He sounded tired and it was difficult to make out the words. Everything happened quickly and the crowd had to stand the entire time. There were no chairs and so only those in the front could see the Pope. After he spoke, the Pope greeted a few school children that were allowed to go to him. It was hard to believe that we were standing there looking at him, inside our school, in our refugee camp. Wow!

Then it was over and the Pope was leaving the school. I finished another roll of film. Although the importance and significance of his being there wasn't diminished, we all were disappointed that the Pope spoke along the lines of improving the living conditions of the refugees versus our right of return.

Sure, we knew the Pope wasn't going to say what we wanted to hear but following his remark at Manger Square in Bethlehem earlier in the day, we thought that maybe, just maybe the Pope would make a clear call for the right of return. In his speech at Manger Square, the Pope had said that, "In the international forum, my predecessors and I have repeatedly proclaimed that there would be no end to the sad conflict in the Holy Land without stable guarantees for the rights of all the peoples involved, on the basis of international law and the relevant United Nations resolutions and declarations." We had hoped that in his speech in Dheisheh, he would be more precise. He wasn't.

As the Pope, Arafat and their entourage started driving away, the press began interviewing camp residents, to get their reactions. Bit by bit, the press started leaving too.

The crowd started leaving slowly but there were still hundreds of people out on the Jerusalem–Hebron road. As my friends and I stood out on the street trying to decide whether to go to Bethlehem for a bite to eat or stick around the camp, a scuffle started a few feet away from us. We got closer to see what was happening, and it looked like there was some kind of a brawl between a policeman and a young camp resident. Several people were trying to contain the incident, trying to get people to disperse. But very suddenly, things seemed to get out of hand. An officer or a policeman took off his belt and attempted to hit a youth. This was when the crowd started getting restless. The mood in the camp had been a bit tense shortly before the Pope's arrival. Jibril Rjoub, the head of the Palestinian Preventive Security in the West Bank, had ordered the arrest of some activists from the Popular Front for the Liberation of Palestine, after some members of the PFLP hung posters of the group's leader, George Habash. This hardly was a reason to arrest anyone, but the head of Preventive Security was apparently adamant on making some arrests. He ordered his men to confiscate an activist's identification papers, and it appeared that once the Pope had completed his visit, some arrests were going to be made.

Word of this had quickly spread around the camp, explaining the tension in the atmosphere following the brawl with the policeman. All of a sudden, and without warning, the crowd started running in our direction. Loren, Mary and I started running too. We took shelter in a nearby shop right inside the entrance of the camp as stones began flying into the air. Then the crowd started moving back out on the main street. We followed to watch.

The place was suddenly swarming with police and security. Unbelievable! The police were throwing stones at the people and the people were throwing stones back. Everyone was shouting. It was so out of control. Tens and tens of policemen stood next to each other along the width of the street, wielding their batons in a face-off with the crowd. The stones kept flying in the air. Some police officers at the scene were beating fellow policemen on their legs with their batons, trying to force them back. Similarly, many men from the camp where trying to get the crowd of people to move back.

The effort to put an end to the stone throwing was being made by individuals on both sides.

But the stone throwing persisted. The stoning from the crowds would force the police to retreat down the street and then the stoning of the police would force the crowd to retreat inside the camp. This kept going on, back and forth. My friends and I were out on the street, in the middle of it all. We kept running back and forth on the main road, hiding whenever the stones flew overheard. It was the Intifada revisited. But it was also very sad. The policemen, mostly young men from Gaza, are sons of the Intifada, and so was the crowd from the camp. To watch Palestinians fighting against fellow Palestinians was very disheartening. Women came out of their houses and started urging the police to move back. And all along, there were individuals on both sides trying to calm the situation by trying, but not succeeding, in pulling people back.

We saw people and policemen bend over as they were hit by stones. The police were viciously striking people with their batons. We could see a group of anti-riot forces, wearing helmets and shields, try to sneak into the camp. Dusk had already turned to dark. The shouts from the crowd inside the camp were getting louder and louder and more and more camp residents were turning up. This was a battle between civilians and the police, and everyone came out to defend the camp. The police were throwing stones at the houses adjacent to the entrance as well as hurling stones inside the camp.

Then suddenly, the crowd let out what sounded like a unanimous loud shout and came dashing out of the camp all at once. The police started running down the street and the crowd ran after them, and after them until they got to the eastern edge of the camp.

Even though the police station is up the hill adjacent to the camp, it took more than an hour and a half of riots before an order was finally issued to the police to withdraw. Why did it take this long? No one knows. But it seemed that if the police had been pulled out right away, the riots would have ended much sooner.

After the police withdrew, the main Jerusalem–Hebron road parallel to Dheisheh was packed with people. Some residents from the nearby Aida and Azza Refugee Camps came to show solidarity with Dheisheh as well as some residents from the Bedouin village of Ta'amreh in eastern Bethlehem. The sound of machine-gun fire filled the air. Shots were being fired in the air to celebrate the fact that the police had pulled back. Dance and song circles sprung up here and there. The atmosphere turned into one of celebration. The Pope's visit was all forgotten. Instead, everyone was talking about the battle with the police.

But the celebrations were short-lived. Word suddenly spread that some people had been arrested and everyone started walking up the hill toward the police station. Stones were hurled at the station as unidentified individuals approached the police station from the back entrance and fired shots. We heard shots off and on and then the ambulances started going back and forth. Luckily, no one was injured in the shooting.

But all the injuries, 57 altogether, were either from stones or police brutality. One 16-year-old boy from the camp sustained a broken nose, a broken arm, a bruised eye and a cut in his leg. He said he was beaten up by 20 policemen, lost consciousness in the process and came to at the police station.

The police also raided the hospital where the injured were being treated and beat up more Dheisheh people there, including camp residents who work for various security forces. Local activists from the camp, as well as members of the different security forces who are also from the camp, quickly intervened to contain the incident. Their efforts were tremendous.

Political activists, representing various political factions, received blows with batons and stones as they tried to stop the riot. Everyone intervened to bring the sad events to an end.

A meeting was held at my house and a follow-up committee was set up to investigate. The committee issued a press release, holding the chief of police responsible because he issued orders to the police to storm the camp.

The traffic lights that were finally installed near our entrance a day before the Pope's visit were smashed during the riots and the main road looks like a battlefield. Stones cover the pavement and sidewalks.

This incident brings home, to each and every one of us here, the importance of building a civil society in Palestine. Our policemen aren't Israelis; they aren't the occupation. Rather, they are our brothers, our sons and our husbands. They are, in short, our people. And it has to be different with them. It has to be. It is the only way we can survive as a society and the only way we can have a future. Because in the end, when Dheisheh came under attack, no one cared who the attackers were. The entire camp, with all its different political factions, came out to defend itself.

The funny thing is that on the day of the Pope's arrival, ABC *Nightly News* called me to say that the show's famous anchor, Peter Jennings, would be in Dheisheh and wanted to interview me. Having studied Radio and Television at college and having always wanted to work as a TV correspondent, Peter Jennings is one of those news people I had always wanted to meet. I did. He's a great interviewer, the sort who acts human and puts you at ease. But meeting him wasn't the highlight of my day. Nor, for that matter, was the long-awaited Pope's visit. Rather, the highlight was seeing fellow refugees in Dheisheh come together to fight back against police brutality. They did it with incredible dignity and an unquestionable sense of pride. It was great to see people so unwilling to take any crap from anyone, even the Palestinian Authority.

*   *   *

Pope's Address in Dheisheh Refugee Camp
Wednesday, March 22, 2000

Dear Friends, Dear brothers and sisters the refugees:

It is important to me that my pilgrimage to the birthplace of Jesus Christ, on this the two thousandth anniversary of that extraordinary event includes this visit to Dheisheh. It is deeply significant that here, close to Bethlehem, I am meeting you, refugees and displaced persons, and representatives of the organizations and agencies involved in a true mission of mercy. Throughout my pontificate I have felt close to the Palestinian people in their sufferings.

I greet each one of you, and I hope and pray that my visit will bring some comfort in your difficult situation. Please God it will help to draw attention to your continuing plight. You have been deprived of many things, which represent basic needs of the human person: proper housing, health care, education and work. Above all you bear the sad memory of what you were forced to leave behind, not just material possessions, but your freedom, the closeness of relatives, and the familial surroundings and cultural traditions, which nourished your personal and family life. It is true that much is being done here in Dheisheh and in other camps to respond to your needs, especially through the United Nations Relief and Works Agency. I am particularly pleased at the effectiveness of the presence of the Pontifical Mission for Palestine and many other Catholic organizations. But there is still much to be done.

The degrading conditions in which refugees often have to live; the continuation over long periods of situations that are barely tolerable in emergencies or for a brief time of transit; the fact that displaced persons are obliged to remain for years in settlement camps: these are the measure of the urgent need for a just solution to the underlying causes of the problem. Only a resolute effort on the part of leaders in the Middle East and in the international community as a whole – inspired by a higher vision of politics as service of the common good – can remove the causes of your present situation. My appeal is for greater international solidarity and the political will to meet this challenge. I plead with all who are sincerely working for justice and peace not to lose heart. I appeal to political leaders to implement agreements already arrived at, and to go forward towards the peace for which all reasonable men and women yearn, to the justice to which they have an inalienable right.

Dear young people, continue to strive through education to take your rightful place in society, despite the difficulties and handicaps that you have to face because of your refugee status. The Catholic Church is particularly happy to serve the noble cause of education through the extremely valuable work of Bethlehem University, founded as a sequel to the visit of my predecessor Pope Paul VI in 1964.

Dear refugees, do not think that your present condition makes you any less important in God's eyes! Never forget your dignity as his children! Here at Bethlehem the Divine child was laid in a manger in a stable; shepherds from the nearby fields, the shepherds who were your ancestors, were the first to receive the heavenly message of peace and hope for the world. God's design was fulfilled in the midst of humility and poverty.

Dear aid workers and volunteers, believe in the task that you are fulfilling! Genuine and practical solidarity with those in need is not a favor conceded, it is a demand of our shared humanity and a recognition of the dignity of every human being. Let us all turn with confidence to the Lord, asking him to inspire those in a position of responsibility to promote justice, security and peace, without delay and in an eminently practical way.

The Church, through her social and charitable organizations, will continue to be at your side and to plead your cause before the world.

Index

Compiled by Auriol Griffith-Jones